Studies in Rhetorics and Feminisms

Series Editors, Cheryl Glenn and Shirley Wilson Logan

RHETORICS OF MOTHERHOOD

Lindal Buchanan

With a Foreword by Amber Kinser

Southern Illinois University Press
Carbondale and Edwardsville

16 15 14 13   4 3 2 1

Cover design and illustration: Fairfax Buchanan-Banks

Library of Congress Cataloging-in-Publication Data
Buchanan, Lindal, date
Rhetorics of motherhood / Lindal Buchanan.
p. cm. — (Studies in rhetorics and feminisms)
Includes bibliographical references and index.
  ISBN 978-0-8093-3220-5 (pbk. : alk. paper)
  ISBN 0-8093-3220-5 (pbk. : alk. paper)
  ISBN 978-0-8093-3221-2 (ebook)
  ISBN 0-8093-3221-3 (ebook)
1. Women—Language. 2. Feminist literary criticism.
3. Motherhood. 4. Rhetoric—Social aspects. 5. Feminist
theory. 6. Historiography—Social aspects.
I. Title.
P120.W66B83 2013
306.44′082—dc23   2012035849

Printed on recycled paper.♻
The paper used in this publication meets the mini-
mum requirements of American National Standard for
Information Sciences—Permanence of Paper for Printed
Library Materials, ANSI Z39.48-1992. ♾

To my foremothers . . .

The myth of eternally changeless motherhood is a central pillar upholding patriarchal privilege; it is part of the assumption everywhere implicit in contemporary Western societies that motherhood is somehow more "natural" and "instinctual" than fatherhood (which has long been recognized as a fluid, socially constructed category, available for legal and philosophical theorizing and practical revision). . . . [M]otherhood, far from a static, "natural" experience, is a moving plurality of potential behaviors always undergoing supervision, revision, and contest, constructed in particularity.

       —Toni Bowers, *The Politics of Motherhood*

Certainly it is possible to theorize women's situations and experiences, or to theorize gender, in ways that minimize the issue of mothering, or do not address it at all. But assumptions about women's mothering are so deeply embedded in U.S. society and culture and are so complexly intertwined with other fundamental beliefs and values that these assumptions are likely to be implicit in accounts of women's situations and experiences and in theories of gender that do not explicitly address mothering.

    —Patrice DiQuinzio, *The Impossibility of Motherhood*

Whether I'm a mother or not, the always obvious fact that I am from the mother half of humanity conditions my life.

       —Ann Snitow, "A Gender Diary"

Contents

Illustrations

Clever Deployments
A Foreword

Few among us are immune to the psychological tugs of what Lindal Buchanan calls the motherhood code. In fact, few of any ilk are immune to it. We get pulled into its emotional force, or we are repositioned by or push against those who are so pulled. When people think, and rhetors speak, of motherhood, they call forth widely shared cultural codes that operate in tension with each other, expanding women's political voice and igniting social change but also reifying gendered norms that contract and attenuate women's agency and possibility. Motherhood is indeed "slippery rhetorical terrain" that proves, at turns, to open up and close off possibilities for creating cultural meaning, determining personal rights, and defining social responsibility.

We do seem to have a bit of an infatuation with motherhood and, for the most part, we don't like to think of it as a strategy, of employing it adroitly to achieve particular social or personal ends or, more accurately but perhaps less palatably, deploying it to achieve them. But there is no doubt, and Buchanan exemplifies it beautifully here, that motherhood is being deployed and people can either figure out how to initiate and fuel their own deployments or they can agree to be positioned within range of others.' The current political climate, with its two-person paradigm of pregnancy (which Buchanan also explains in this book) and fetal ultrasound bills, already has me rethinking my own language. The technologies with which we have medically and otherwise regarded and surveyed pregnancy over the last fifty years, and the ways that antiabortion rhetoric has appropriated them, have profoundly altered how we think about pregnancy and personhood. We had legally and philosophically long held to a view of gestation as a formative, pre-person fetal period experienced and attended to by the mother-as-person. Now, however, we confront impressions of pregnancy as comprising two independent persons, despite fetal dependence on the mother, with such impressions in fact foregrounding the baby over the mother. Having read *Rhetorics of Motherhood*, I am further called to consider anew how my own arguments about women's agency and selfhood may in fact feed the positions I wish to critique more than they fuel the changes I seek to drive. My reckoning here reminds me of my laments about parents who don't want to talk with their children about sex explicitly because they don't want their children thinking about "that" yet. They're already thinking about "that," I say. They have no choice but to think about it since sexual texts everywhere surround them. They already are in dialogue about it. You can join that dialogue and play a part in shaping it or you can choose to be omitted from the conversation, and from much more, for that matter. What Buchanan offers us here is related. The discussion about reproductive rights already is being led by an emphasis on maternal rhetorics, so we can either play a part in shaping those rhetorics or we can choose to be omitted from their conversations, and from much more, for that matter.

Those of us who adopted "pro-choice" arguments wanted to push hard against empty sentimentality about motherhood and contest the erasure of women-as-persons by notions of "life" abstracted and inequitably actuated without regard for life lived. We quite justifiably wanted to fight for reproductive liberty as if women mattered, as if their lives and their desires and their purposeful decisions counted, as if "woman" was not a monolith. In our struggle, we accepted and even fortified a rhetorical distance from motherhood. But, as Buchanan points out, we have failed to tap into its potential for elevated status and rhetorical force, given how motherhood functions, to use Richard Weaver's notion, as a "god term," which renders all other models for talking about pregnancy, and children, and their care subordinate at best and damning at worst. As a consequence of having set up this distance, we are finding that reproductive freedom rhetoric operates now with severely and increasingly restricted currency. In fact, we are finding that our very discourse is being effectively dismantled and reconstructed to support structures antithetical to our purposes. Consider for example pre-abortion fetal ultrasound requirements, which, at this writing, are required in seven U.S. states. Couched in terms of the pregnant woman's "right to know" and informed decision-making, the legislative and public rhetoric in support of these unnecessary procedures has deployed mother/child images characteristic of the political right and antiabortion rights rhetoric and has simultaneously co-opted arguments about information access that have been historically core to the left. That is, in their fevered effort to chip away at *Roe v. Wade*, not to mention *Griswold v. Connecticut*, abortion rights opponents and, more recently, contraception opponents, have been dexterous in their use of a variety of arguments. It would behoove reproductive self-determination proponents to be as agile and shrewd. Buchanan argues that claims about supporting reproductive freedom and agency that are aligned with, rather than distanced from, the language and imagery of mothers and children are likely to operate with more persuasive force because they tap into "maternity's rich valences" and they meet audiences where they already are—at least compelled by mother/child language and images, and more likely rather intoxicated by them.

Inspired by my read of *Rhetorics of Motherhood* to reconfigure how I talk about reproductive rights, I wrote a piece for my weekly blog, *Thursdays with Dr. Mama*, titled "Reproductive Wrongs." My goal as I wrote the piece was to begin training myself to talk about abortion rights in ways that didn't quash mother/child imagery. At the end of the post, I had, in fact, quashed that very thing. I posted a piece that focused on women and rights and did little to employ representations that would tap into public intoxications with mothers and children. I am finding the task of reconceiving my own position to be a challenging, though I'll concede necessary, one.

Still, maternal rhetoric is polyvalent. Mother rhetors will often appease audiences somehow, evoking familiar images for women's identities and social place that are socially constructed as, Buchanan explains, "natural, eternal, and timeless." And women can use this audience-assuring "maternal ethos" to great advantage as they work to pivot social practices. Buchanan details how Margaret Sanger's strategic use of motherhood in this way redirected public and political attention away from her more controversial activities and rendered her birth control activism concedable and even credible. But it could go a whole other way. A woman's full selfhood can also be eclipsed by her role as mother in the public imagination, or by assumptions that she should be a mother, so being more shrewd won't just mean using some of the language and images of those who would have women saddled with the lifelong impacts of a fertility that is unrestricted, or would subsume "woman" under "mother." Buchanan also explores how Diane Nash's use of motherhood as a way of justifying some of the choices she made in her civil rights work, and the choice to go to jail while pregnant in particular, was responded to in ways that effectively erased her legitimate place in civil rights history. So being shrewd won't just mean foregrounding or revering motherhood. Approaching things this narrowly might well do more to further constrain women than to secure or maintain their right to full person-hood. But feminist and women activists have a long history, as I discuss in *Motherhood and Feminism*, of deploying maternal rhetorics in a variety of ways—to leverage other arguments, critique social structure, recon-ceptualize family forms, celebrate mothering experience, for example. We are being called to reimagine, once again, how we think about the relationship between womanhood and motherhood and we are called to do it in child-centric times that opaque the bodily integrity and per-sonhood of women. Though these times may get worse before they get better, we will move from here as we have so many times before if we are willing to be rhetorically inventive, resourceful, and clever.

Amber Kinser
Department of Communication
East Tennessee State University

Preface

Discourses about mothers, mothering, and motherhood permeate U.S. political culture and are employed by both women and men in order to advance themselves and their agendas within the public realm. These discourses, however, prove to be slippery rhetorical terrain for women, on the one hand, affording them authority and credibility but, on the other, positioning them disadvantageously within the gendered status quo. *Rhetorics of Motherhood* examines that paradox by detailing the cultural construction and persuasive operations of the Mother within American public discourse; tracing its use and impact in three case studies; and theorizing how, when, and why maternal discourse works to women's benefit or detriment.

Chapter 1, "Theorizing Motherhood in Public Discourse," explores historic, semiotic, ideological, and rhetorical dimensions of the Mother, a construct that encodes dominant beliefs, values, and assumptions about the role. Given its entrenchment within systems of gender, knowledge, and power and its familiarity to cultural insiders, the Mother is easily invoked but difficult to resist in rhetorical situations. I present a framework that explains the construct's current signification as well as its capacity both to aid and to undermine women. The code of motherhood circulates widely in American culture, at once influencing social expectations of and ignoring critical differences among women and their mothering practices. The chapter, therefore, also addresses how subjects' intersectional identities and social locations inform maternal goals and performances and investigates the reciprocal influence of practice upon constructs of motherhood and vice versa.

Chapter 1, then, prepares the ground for the project by detailing how motherhood invokes a shared cultural code and generates powerful persuasive resources that reinforce gender stereotypes and diminish women's complexity, dimensions, and opportunities. Chapters 2, 3, and 4 present case studies that explore these tensions. Spanning the early twentieth to the early twenty-first century, they focus respectively on the issues of birth control, civil rights, and reproductive choice and track how motherhood has been employed rhetorically to advance feminist, resistant, and conservative ends. These cases illustrate the diverse forms that maternal appeals can take—whether physically embodied through pregnancy and progeny or communicated verbally, visually, or performatively—and trace their impact on women's political goals and civic standing.

Chapter 2, "From 'Wild Woman Writer' to 'Mother of Two': Margaret Sanger, Birth Control, and Ethos Repair," examines the controversial activist at the start of her rhetorical career (1914–17), focusing on her appropriation of motherhood to repair damaged ethos and develop a widespread movement for contraception. While working as a maternity nurse in New York's Lower East Side, Sanger first encountered the constraints imposed by the Comstock laws, which prohibited medical professionals from discussing (much less providing patients with) birth control. Convinced that working-class women desperately needed such information, she began to publish accessible explanations of human anatomy, reproduction, and pregnancy prevention, efforts that led to her eventual indictment on "obscenity" charges and flight from the country to escape prosecution. After her return from exile, Sanger devoted herself to repairing her tarnished ethos, to establishing a strong base of support for challenging the Comstock laws, and to placing the issue of birth control on the national agenda. Maternal rhetoric enabled her to accomplish each of these objectives. It afforded her means for reformulating her public image, encouraging women's identification, creating exigency for contraception, and inspiring action to change its legal, medical, and social standing. Motherhood enabled the rhetor to reposition herself and her cause from "the radical margins to mainstream respectability" and to forward the feminist agenda of giving women reproductive control (Katz xxiii). At the same time, Sanger's maternal framework foregrounded the interests of white, married, elite women and elided those of immigrant women, women of color, and unmarried women. Aligning birth control with motherhood, then, came at a cost—sacrificing the contraceptive needs and objectives of far too many women for far too long. The strategy's results, however, were also substantial, contributing to the creation of a legal and social environment that respected women's regulation of their own fertility. Both aspects of maternal rhetoric—its sights and blindnesses, its advantages and shortcomings—are at the heart of this chapter.

Chapter 3, "Motherhood, Civil Rights, and Remembrance: Recuperating Diane Nash," centers on a neglected leader of the early civil-rights movement who, while still in her early twenties, guided the Nashville student sit-ins to a successful conclusion, helped found the Student Non-violent Coordinating Committee, and revived the Freedom Rides after violence threatened to end them. In 1961, Nash moved to Mississippi to coordinate the Rides, and her workshops on nonviolent resistance soon led to charges of "contributing to the delinquency of minors," resulting in hefty fines and a two-year jail term. Although a legal challenge of the sentence was underway, she elected to revoke her appeal and enter prison in order to alter movement policy and persuade arrested protesters to stop posting bail and to stay in jail. Six-months pregnant at the time, Nash employed maternal appeals brilliantly (if briefly) in a press release and letter to civil-rights workers that detailed economic, philosophical, and policy reasons for her action: "I believe that if I go to jail now it may help hasten that day when my child and all children will be free—not only on the day of their birth but for all of their lives" ("Message" 1). Her rhetorical use of motherhood was so moving, in fact, that it subsequently became the centerpiece of historical accounts of the event and completely displaced the principles and objectives underlying her resistant action. Furthermore, these depictions commemorated Nash as a mother rather than a strategist and seriously compromised her rightful place in civil-rights history; only recently have feminist scholars begun to recuperate the reasons underlying her action and argue convincingly for her leadership role in the movement. The chapter's examination of Nash's appeal revocation, of subsequent representations of the rhetor and event, and of historical remembrance interrogates motherhood's paradoxical impact on women, affording them potent persuasive means while also constraining them in public life and cultural memory.

Motherhood is contextually defined, contingent, and changeable, its associations forever in flux rather than fixed. The maternal body, likewise, lacks stable, inherent meaning and is, instead, constantly (re)formulated through scientific, medical, legal, political, and popular discourse. The final case study tracks recent advances in imaging technology and their influence on rhetorical figurations of motherhood, focusing, in particular, on the ways they have been used to advance antiabortion policies and politics. Chapter 4, "Changing Constructs of Motherhood: Pregnancy and Personhood in Laci and Conner's Law," focuses on congressional deliberation over a 2003 crime bill that introduced fetal personhood into federal law for the first time and, thus, helped to establish legal precedent for overturning *Roe v. Wade*. I concentrate specifically on rhetorical depictions of pregnancy, which has been recast from a holistic, gestational process unfolding within a woman's body into an uneasy cohabitation of two legal subjects—the fetus and its female host—with potentially conflicting rights. Conservatives' figuration of the maternal body led to passage of a law that, ironically, has the long-term potential to jeopardize women's control over when or whether to become mothers. Further, the political repercussions of congressional members' rhetoric extends far beyond one piece of legislation and instead carries troubling implications for the likelihood of sustaining safe, legal abortion in America and protecting women's reproductive rights from further erosion.

Chapters 2, 3, and 4 examine how motherhood provides rhetors with gendered means for advancing feminist, resistant, and regressive goals. In the conclusion, I reflect upon the lessons learned about maternal rhetorics from the case studies and identify additional lines of inquiry for those interested in exploring the topic further. I hope my endeavor inspires others to study motherhood's construction, application, and implications in new rhetorical situations and gain additional insight into the construct's variability and vulnerability to change.

Acknowledgments

A great many friends and colleagues have contributed to the creation of *Rhetorics of Motherhood*. First and foremost, I'm grateful to Cheryl Glenn and Shirley Wilson Logan, editors of the Studies in Rhetorics and Feminisms Series, for their guidance and patience as I focused and developed the manuscript. Deep appreciation goes, too, to my dear friend Paul Butler, who has provided me a ready ear, moral support, and invaluable feedback over the years. I have benefited as well from the wise counsel and insightful readings of Cynthia Lewiecki-Wilson, Kim Harrison, David Metzger, and Carol Mattingly, all of whom helped to sharpen my analysis and argument in significant ways.

Other talented, capable, and generous individuals also assisted in the development and production of this project. Librarian Bruce Dietz of Kettering University proved an indefatigable and creative researcher, obtaining hard-to-find sources that proved central to my study. Meanwhile, Amber Kinser, whose scholarship on motherhood I admire greatly, wrote a thoughtful, provocative foreword to the manuscript. I also appreciate funding provided by Charles Wilson, dean of Arts and Letters at Old Dominion University, who graciously underwrote the costs of permissions and indexing. As always, the accomplished staff at Southern Illinois University Press was wonderful to work with, particularly acquisitions editor Kristine Priddy and production manager Barb Martin. My gifted daughter, Fairfax Buchanan-Banks, created the beautiful cover of this book, capturing in striking visual terms the discursive elements of motherhood and womanhood that I examine in its pages.

Finally, on a personal note, I thank my family for its faith and support—Fairfax, Rochelle, Fay, Colleen, Walter, Bruce, Angie, Brett, Stephanie, Andrew, Brian, Emily, Ashley, Jack, and Luke. Last, and most important of all, I am blessed with a remarkable husband, Don Davis, whose love, humor, balance, and encouragement make the rough places smooth each and every day.

Rhetorics of Motherhood

1

Theorizing Motherhood in Public Discourse

The person I'm about to introduce to you was . . . a concerned
citizen who became a member of the PTA, then a city council
member, and then a mayor, and now a governor who beat the
long odds to win a tough election on a message of reform and
public integrity. And, I am especially proud to say in the week we
celebrate the anniversary of women's suffrage, a devoted wife and
a mother of five.

—John McCain

When presidential hopeful John McCain surprised party and political
pundits by announcing that a relatively unknown Alaska governor
would serve as his running mate, Sarah Palin entered history, becoming
the first female vice-presidential candidate on a Republican ticket. Her
electrifying address to the Republican National Convention (RNC)
marked her first solo foray onto the national stage and covered expected
ground—praising McCain's character and experience, detailing her own
political accomplishments and qualifications, attacking the Democratic
nominee for president, and forecasting Republican victory come November. Palin also made some decidedly unconventional moves, most
notably, foregrounding motherhood to demonstrate fitness for public
office. Her strategy was surprising, first, because maternity is not
normally equated with political authority in America and, second,
because highlighting it runs counter to female candidates' typical self-
fashioning, which plays "down their softer, domestic side" and plays
"up their toughness" (Toner, n.p.). Palin devoted considerable time
to family in her speech, not only introducing her husband, children,
parents, and siblings but also describing life as a working mother and
governor ("Convention Speech"). Discussing two children, in particular,
paid handsome dividends for the candidate: Her eldest son's imminent

departure for Iraq with the army infantry showcased maternal pride and patriotism while her youngest son's diagnosis of Down syndrome added poignancy and credence to her promised advocacy for special-needs children. Palin dedicated nearly a fifth of her address to family matters and explicitly identified herself as a mother four times, most memorably as a "hockey mom" or pit bull with lipstick, an image that provocatively blended ferocity with femininity and suggested she would be as tough and tenacious in office as any man. What is more, the candidate's rhetorical invocation of motherhood continued after the speech's conclusion when she was joined onstage by her husband and five children. Palin took son Trig from her husband's arms and awkwardly positioned the child to face the audience, crafting visual rhetoric that reinforced maternal ethos and communicated a pro-life message to viewers (see Figure 1.1). After all, Palin had refused to terminate her pregnancy after testing

Figure 1.1. Vice-presidential candidate Sarah Palin shows Trig to the nation (2008). Reuters/Mike Segar.

positive for Down syndrome, so Trig physically embodied his mother's convictions.[1] Cumulatively, these references to family, children, and motherhood enabled the vice-presidential aspirant to craft engaging, credible, trustworthy character and to infuse her remarks with passion.

Palin's impressive debut before a national audience suggests that motherhood is still golden in the public forum—even in the twenty-first century. Over the course of her RNC appearance, motherhood served as a rhetorical topos, "a location or space in an art where a speaker can look for 'available means of persuasion,'" according to George Kennedy (in Aristotle 45). It generated a rich assortment of appeals that Palin delivered verbally (during her address), visually and performatively (during her onstage interactions with her children), and corporeally (during Trig's introduction to viewers). However, in addition to functioning as a topos, motherhood operated on an ideological level as well: Palin's self-presentation as a prototypical mother brought thoughts of love, care, children, protection, morality, self-sacrifice, home, and nation to the minds of the audience.

To help unpack motherhood's multiple layers of meaning on this occasion, I turn to Roland Barthes's indispensable exploration of first- and second-order signification (or denotation and connotation). He distinguishes between a literal, denotative level and an abstract, connotative level that taps into overarching cultural constructs. Barthes teases out these distinct planes of signification in his famous analysis of *Paris-Match* magazine (see Figure 1.2):

> On the cover, a young Negro in a French uniform is saluting, with his eyes uplifted, probably fixed on a fold of the tricolor. All this is the *meaning* of the picture. But, whether naively or not, I see very well what it signifies to me: that France is a great Empire, that all her sons, without any colour discrimination, faithfully serve under her flag, and that there is no better answer to the detractors of an alleged colonialism than the zeal shown by this Negro in serving his so-called oppressors. (*Mythologies* 116)

The first order of signification denotes a young soldier of color saluting the French flag while the second order extends and complicates the message through connotations of "Frenchness" and "Militariness." Although the denotative soldier persists as a "rich, fully experienced, spontaneous, innocent, *indisputable* image," connotation aligns him with nationalistic ideals, values, and assumptions regarding France's greatness and capacity to inspire the admiration, loyalty, and devotion of colonized subjects.

The literal soldier, while not erased, is "tamed, put at a distance, made almost transparent; it recedes a little, it becomes the accomplice of a concept which comes to it fully armed, French imperiality" (118). The image, thus, speaks to viewers on two levels simultaneously, a complex form of signification that produces "rapid alternation" between first and second orders of meaning and the "constant game of hide-and-seek" that lies at the heart of connotation. (Barthes, by the way, used many different terms for second-order signification over the course of his career, including *connotation*, *myth*, *ideology*, and *cultural code*. I employ the terms *cultural code*, *code*, or the capitalized *Mother* when referring to this level of meaning.)

Barthes's method of interpretation is useful for reading the image of Palin and Trig in Figure 1.1. At the denotative level, a female candidate holds her son while, at the connotative level, she instantiates the cultural

Figure 1.2. Cover of *Paris Match* (no. 326: Les Nuits de L'Armée). Paris Match/Scoop.

ideal of the Mother and taps into a web of positive associations that adds depth, richness, and texture to the visual message. Invoking motherhood in this manner has real rhetorical benefits for Palin, enabling her to establish strong ethos and to connect emotionally with voters, especially those who also oppose abortion. At the same time, it also constrains her, a paradox that stems from the construct's place within the gender system. A cultural code (such as motherhood) communicates but cloaks prevailing power relations; through constant repetition, it makes those relations seem normal, eternal, objective, self-evident expressions of "the way things are" (Barthes, *S/Z* 206). The French soldier operates in precisely this fashion, erasing the "contingent," "historical," "*fabricated*, quality of colonialism" and presenting it instead as innocent, inevitable, and factual (Barthes, *Mythologies* 143). The Mother, likewise, alludes to, masks, and sustains the network of power relations that undergird gender. Palin accesses that network through her references to motherhood, summoning shared scripts and beliefs (for instance, that mothers are virtuous, self-sacrificing, noble, and admirable) and enveloping herself in a culturally approved mantle of femininity/maternity. However, the code of motherhood also restricts the candidate through its embedded and inequitable gender presumptions (holding, for example, that mothers belong in the private rather than the public sphere) and thereby undermines her run for political office.

Rhetorics of motherhood, I argue, not only benefit women, giving them authority and credibility, but also impede them, always/already positioning them disadvantageously within the gendered status quo. In coming chapters, I examine rhetors whose persuasive use of motherhood afforded them powerful means for advancing civic agendas and, at the same time, reinforced damaging gender stereotypes harmful to women. The quandary of employing maternal rhetorics, then, is that both their force and peril derive from entrenchment within dominant systems of gender, knowledge, and power. Motherhood, nevertheless, pervades American public discourse and, as Palin's visual argument against abortion suggests, has been skillfully employed in recent decades to advance conservative policies, from defeating the Equal Rights Amendment to eroding *Roe v Wade*.[2] It is important to understand why motherhood has so often worked to women's political detriment and whether it might be applied to different ends. Therefore, the feminist objectives of *Rhetorics of Motherhood* are to explore the discursive construction and persuasive operations of motherhood in public discourse;

to map its rhetorical use and impact in three case studies set in the United States between the early twentieth and twenty-first centuries; and to theorize how, when, and why motherhood works to women's (dis)advantage.

To forward my central claim regarding motherhood's Janus-like capacity to generate compelling persuasive means while buttressing restrictive gender roles, I expand upon its discursive, cultural, and rhetorical construction. Per Michel Foucault, I envision motherhood as part of a vast symbolic order that is comprised of discursive formations, loosely organized bodies of knowledge that establish "regimes of truth," encode power relations, and produce speaking subjects ("Truth and Power" 131). Discursive formations have an epistemic function, marking particular objects as worthy of attention, producing knowledge about those objects, and encouraging acceptance of purported truths about them. These truths are conveyed through cultural codes that both reflect and sustain the dominant systems of knowledge, power, and discourse that comprise the symbolic order (Foucault, *Archeology* 39). The code of motherhood is part of the larger discursive formation of gender and so reiterates its governing constructs of male and female, masculinity and femininity. Due to this placement, the code of motherhood functions as "an abbreviated version of the entire system" of gender (Silverman 31) and brings that system to bear upon subjects, social practices, and rhetorical texts. Like gender, the code is contextually bound; therefore, its constitution varies across time, cultures, locations, and communities. (I flesh out the emergence and evolution of the contemporary code of motherhood later in this chapter.)

Susan Miller's *Trust in Texts: A Different History of Rhetoric* illuminates the interconnections between codes and persuasion and, thus, also pertains to the study of motherhood in public discourse. Subjects, she observes, are educated into a common cultural matrix that establishes shared "ideas about standards of credible behavior," "fitting responses to specific situations," and "appropriate ways of talking about them" (22). These conventions, in turn, promote a sense of community that is based upon emotion and its corollary, trust (23). Therefore, a rhetor must identify scripts, codes, and values capable of inspiring collective feelings (say, of anger, fear, enthusiasm, admiration, and so on) and establishing trust with the audience—all of this *before* persuasion becomes possible. To adapt Miller's insights to the case at hand, motherhood is part of the cultural matrix, and enculturation entails learning standards of credible behavior by and toward mothers; the role's associations, obligations, and values; and appropriate ways of discussing and performing maternity. To those schooled to its cultural place and meaning, the Mother invites—perhaps even commands—prescribed emotional responses, such as respect, obedience, and love. Palin's decision to emphasize motherhood during her RNC appearance resonated deeply with viewers, disposing their feelings favorably and encouraging trust. A code, after all, interpellates subjects, affording them the opportunity to recognize and respond appropriately to dominant scripts and ideologies and, thereby, create socially legible character (Nguyen, n.p.). According to Barthes, a cultural code is imperative, insistent, and unfailingly solicitous; it buttonholes subjects and demands their acknowledgement and acquiescence: "It is *I* whom it has come to seek. It is turned towards me, I am subjected to its intentional force, it summons me to receive its expansive ambiguity" (*Mythologies* 124). Due to its role in subject formation and collusion with the gender system, the Mother is easy to invoke but difficult to resist. When it surfaces in a rhetorical text, the code of motherhood (re)interpellates the audience, placing members in familiar subject positions, eliciting conventional feelings, and inspiring trust.

The Mother not only encourages identification and a predetermined emotional response but also discourages critical distance, in effect shutting down analysis, discussion, deliberation, reflection, and nuance. This was apparent when Palin presented Trig to the nation: Maternal connotation made the mother and child inviolable and dictated audience allegiance and respect. While it was possible to disagree with and debate Palin's stance on abortion, it was virtually impossible to contest her visual rhetoric without appearing loutish and insensitive. The candidate's invocation of motherhood tapped into the overarching system of gender and made her appeal difficult to refuse or refute directly, lending support to Daniel Chandler's observation that resisting a message is far easier than resisting a dominant code (188). The Mother's persuasive force, then, stems from its place within the gender hierarchy and cultural matrix, its capacity to stir emotion and inspire trust, and its ability to encourage acquiescence and mute critique and reflection.

To understand the code in rhetorical terms and appreciate its impact in public discourse, one must recollect motherhood's exalted status in American society. According to Judith Warner, Americans' veneration is so strong that it approaches the status of religion, investing maternity "with quasi-ecclesiastical notions of Good and Evil" (706). If motherhood represents Good, however, it requires an antithesis to represent Evil, a reciprocal relationship captured in Richard Weaver's notion of *god* and *devil terms*. Weaver contends that societies make sense of the world by discerning (I would say by agreeing upon) rhetorical absolutes like good and evil; they then use these absolutes to sort objects and experiences, to evaluate them and create hierarchies, and to systematize relationships between attractive and repulsive terms.[3] A *god term* is an ultimate expression to which all others are subordinate; god terms establish the scale of comparison and thus diminish the force of other terms (Weaver 212). They also encapsulate ideas and ideals that subjects feel "socially impelled to accept and even to sacrifice for," responses that are sure indicators of god terms, according to Weaver (214). *Devil terms*, meanwhile, are the counterparts of god terms. If god terms attract, then devil terms repulse; if god terms invite approval, then their opposites merit reproach (212). Devil terms fulfill crucial functions, not only providing indispensable contrast with god terms but also affording society external adversaries and internal scapegoats, for "we need the enemy in order to define ourselves" (222).

The Mother, I maintain, operates as a god term within public discourse and connotes a myriad of positive associations, including children, love, protection, home, nourishment, altruism, morality, religion, self-sacrifice, strength, the reproductive body, the private sphere, and the nation. Meanwhile, its corresponding devil term, Woman, invokes negative attributes, such as childlessness, self-centeredness, work, materialism, hysteria, irrationality, the sensual/sexual body, and the public sphere. Woman is the antithesis of Mother—the dark to its light, the failure to its success—and a necessary internal scapegoat. The Woman/Mother continuum presented in the table below captures these distinctions.

The devil-term Woman and god-term Mother are rhetorical expressions of the code of motherhood and overarching system of gender; they provide speakers with immediately recognizable (and culturally resonant) stereotypes, each comprised of well-known qualities and associations. When either figure is invoked, much is suggested even if little is said, an effect produced by embedded gender assumptions that slip silently through what George Yoos calls the gaps, ellipses, and enthymemes of rhetoric. Persuasive appeals, unlike formal logic, do not depend upon what is explicitly stated and instead "sketch the form of their arguments in a context of linguistic, communicative, and cultural presumptions that audiences intuitively grasp" (411). The Woman and Mother are familiar to cultural insiders and, therefore, provide rhetors with opportunities to

Woman (Devil Term)		Mother (God Term)
childlessness		children
work		home
sex		love
self-centeredness	**rhetorics that**	empathy
materialism	**combine**	protection
immorality	**elements**	religion
hysteria	**of the**	nourishment
irrationality	**Woman and**	altruism
extreme emotion	**Mother**	morality
self-indulgence		self-sacrifice
weakness		strength
the sensual body		the reproductive body
the public sphere		the private sphere
		the nation

Table. The Woman/Mother continuum.

employ "what everyone knows" (Miller 67). The availability of these privileged and devalued positions for women creates a shorthand of sorts, enabling speakers to sketch immediately identifiable characters—the sainted mother or selfish career woman—with only a few strokes.[4]

The Mother and Woman afford rhetors means for exalting or denigrating women, as does the terrain that falls between the extremes. To illustrate the rhetorical possibilities of the middle ground, I examine one woman's sanctification and another's degradation through their positioning along the Woman/Mother continuum. Mother Teresa of Calcutta suggests the advantageous possibilities here, her ethos successfully blending elements of both the Woman (childlessness, dedication to work) and Mother (religion, love, selflessness, altruism, compassion). Her titular motherhood produced positive connotations and aligned her with the venerable Catholic Madonna, associations that softened and exonerated her stubborn determination and persistence with popes and heads of state (see Kolodiejchuk). By appropriating and attaching maternal qualities to her efforts, Mother Teresa made her vision for assisting the poor a reality, and she founded an order to continue that work following her death—the Missionaries of Charity, her spiritual children. Her example reveals the rhetorical advantages of positioning a woman close to the Mother end of the continuum.

The reverse, however, also holds true—inching a mother toward the Woman end of the continuum is a sure way to demean her. Such tactics severely tarnished the reputation of murdered civil-rights activist Viola Liuzzo, who left her husband, Detroit home, and children to journey south and join Martin Luther King's five-day march from Selma to Montgomery. Like television viewers across the nation, she was galvanized by images of the "Bloody Sunday" attack on six hundred peaceful activists and inspired to support their protest of racist voter-registration practices. On 25 March 1965, she entered the Alabama state capitol alongside 25,000 marchers, participating in a momentous event in the long campaign for racial equality. Liuzzo's euphoria, however, was short lived: she was shot dead later that same evening by the Ku Klux Klan (Branch, *At Cannan's Edge* 171–88).

Historian Mary Stanton observes that the media initially lauded the murder victim's courage and commitment to social justice but, within days, began to question her fitness as a mother. Stanton attributes the shift to J. Edgar Hoover's initiation of a smear campaign designed to distract the press from the presence of a paid FBI informant among the Klansmen who killed Liuzzo (63). The agency, therefore, leaked distorted and erroneous information, suggesting that Liuzzo was mentally unstable, sexually promiscuous, drug addled, immoral, and, worst of all, a bad mother, and the media accepted much of it uncritically. Consequently, she was depicted as an irresponsible, self-centered, thoughtless, volatile, unbalanced woman who had strayed from her ordained sphere— negative attributes typically associated with the Woman category that enunciated maternal shortcomings. Such attributions ultimately transformed Liuzzo from a civil-rights martyr into an unsympathetic victim who was, first, tarred and feathered rhetorically and then blamed for her own death.[5] "Bad" mothering tarnished Liuzzo's reputation and overshadowed her sacrifice for the movement, a legacy that indicates the dire consequences of positioning a mother on the Woman end of the rhetorical continuum.

The Woman/Mother continuum sheds light on motherhood's cultural construction and rhetorical implications—both positive and negative—for women. In coming chapters, it provides a framework for analyzing motherhood in public discourse and tracing how, why, and when it advances or undermines women's standing. Examining rhetorics of motherhood in this manner has the potential not only to yield insight into the interrelationships among gender, race, class, power, and persuasion but also to integrate women's distinct concerns, experiences, and perspectives into the discipline. In the remainder of this chapter, I continue to lay a foundation for *Rhetorics of Motherhood* by acknowledging feminist rhetorical scholarship and debates that inform my project, by tracing the historical emergence of contemporary constructs of motherhood, and by exploring the code's influence on social practice, institutional policy, and intersectional difference.

Feminist Scholarship on Motherhood

Motherhood has inspired abundant research in fields ranging from film and women's studies to philosophy, literature, and sociology.[6] Rhetoric, however, has only just begun to explore the topic, an oversight likely rooted in the discipline's traditional focus on issues and concerns pertaining to elite male rhetors, who for millennia were its primary students, practitioners, teachers, and theorists. Women may have been excluded from public forums and ignored within the discipline, but they, nevertheless, "thought about, studied, and practiced rhetoric, indirectly for much of western history and, incrementally over the past 350 years, more directly" (Buchanan and Ryan, xvi). Feminist historiographers have begun to excavate this hidden history and retheorize persuasion through the lens of gender, efforts that have produced the burgeoning field of feminist rhetorics (comprised, for the most part, of scholars in departments of English and Communication Studies).[7] Scholarship focusing on the intersections of motherhood and American public discourse in the nineteenth, twentieth, and twenty-first centuries has also been central to *Rhetorics of Motherhood*. In this section, I provide a brief, chronological overview of pertinent research and then discuss a pivotal debate within this emergent area of rhetorical study.

My own *Regendering Delivery: The Fifth Canon and Antebellum Women Rhetors* examines the unique constraints that confronted women who were both mothers and public speakers prior to the Civil War. Chapters 4 and 5 trace maternal rhetors' negotiation of the corporeal realities of pregnancy, their handling of gender assumptions that relegated mothers to private rather than public settings, their resolution of conflicting civic and domestic responsibilities through collaboration, and their efforts to sustain a rhetorical career while bearing and raising children. Also focused on the antebellum period, Leslie Harris's "Motherhood, Race, and Gender: The Rhetoric of Women's Antislavery Activism in the *Liberty Bell* Giftbooks" explores women writers' representations of motherhood as a universal experience and efforts to encourage cross-racial identification on that basis. Giftbook writers emphasized free and enslaved women's shared maternal goals and values as well as critical differences stemming from the "peculiar" institution of slavery, depictions that called for white mothers' commitment to abolition on behalf of disempowered black mothers (295).

Moving forward to the postbellum decades, Nan Johnson devotes a chapter to maternal rhetors in *Gender and Rhetorical Space in American Life, 1866–1910*. She observes that these women routinely reassured the audience they were, first and foremost, able housekeepers, loving wives, and dedicated mothers and, only second, public participants, justifications designed to reconcile unconventional gender and discursive performances with presumed "domestic interests and conventional feminine dispositions" (16). Meanwhile, Mari Boor Tonn's "Militant Motherhood: Labor's Mary Harris 'Mother' Jones" details the late nineteenth-century labor activist's use of maternal ethos and argument. Mother Jones cast workers as her sons and urged them to fight for better working conditions, a strategy that encouraged male identification with the rhetor and proved so successful that it was embraced by other female union organizers (including Ella Reeve "Mother" Bloor, Leanora "Mother" O'Reilly, and Mary "Mother" Skubitz).

Advancing into the twentieth century, Julie Thompson's *Mommy Queerest: Contemporary Rhetorics of Lesbian Maternal Identity* traces the discursive construction of lesbian mothers in the courtroom, the academy, and the media. Thompson uncovers how sexual orientation intersects (and often conflicts) with prevailing beliefs about motherhood in ways that frequently disadvantage lesbian mothers. Feminist scholars Patrice DiQuinzio and Sara Hayden also examine motherhood in contemporary public settings. Both, for example, have published essays on the Million Mom March—a rally in the nation's capital to promote tighter gun-control legislation—and reached opposite conclusions about the effectiveness of the group's maternal rhetorics.

Their debate revolves around motherhood's collusion with the dominant system of gender and whether or not that relationship taints maternal appeals, making them inevitably disadvantageous for women. As this question is pertinent to my own analysis in *Rhetorics of Motherhood*, I explore their divergent viewpoints more thoroughly below.

As the event's name suggests, motherhood was central to participants' identities and political efforts during the 2000 Million Mom March (MMM). It is, therefore, not surprising to learn that marchers regularly invoked *maternalism*, a highly effective discourse developed by nineteenth-century women that "accepted, even idealized, [their] traditional role as wife and mother" while also insisting "that women had a duty to extend their female skills and concerns beyond their own home" (Clapp 3–4). Women rhetors, both then and now, have often appropriated motherhood and used it as both "a motivation and a means" for justifying their efforts in "masculine" public spaces. In "Love and Reason in the Public Sphere: Maternalist Civic Engagement and the Dilemma of Difference," DiQuinzio argues that the MMM's protest played into damaging maternal stereotypes that ultimately undermined the group's political agenda. Media representations of "enraged mothers, like the traditional image of the fierce mother lion protecting her cubs," suggested that their response to gun-related violence was "instinctual and emotion-driven, rather than the result of reasoned analysis," depictions that cast the marchers as hysterical and irrational women (232). The MMM's maternalist discourse also perpetuated essentialist assumptions that link women to children and caretaking, reified spatial arrangements that position mothers in the domestic realm and discourage their political participation, and produced a number of significant erasures, for example, that women are also victims of gun violence and that marchers had not only maternal but also "professional and occupational experience, expertise, and authority" (230). From DiQuinzio's perspective, maternalism yields persuasive means so imbued with gender bias that they typically work to women's detriment and are, therefore, better left alone.

While acknowledging that motherhood can "reinforce problematic gender norms" and "be strategically ineffective" in certain situations, Hayden reaches a different conclusion regarding its rhetorical value in "Family Metaphors and the Nation: Promoting a Politics of Care through the Million Mom March." She argues that MMM participants consistently stressed maternal priorities and experiences in order to promote "alternate modes of political reasoning" that privilege "caring, empathy, and nurturance"

(203, 198). Motherhood, thus, provided women with ethical grounds and rhetorical means for reshaping the existing order; what is more, in advocating publicly for social change, marchers redefined conventional motherhood, "unmooring" it from "essentialist foundations" and transforming it into a source of civic strength and political power (209). Hayden concludes that the cultural construct of motherhood is being actively and positively reformed through the MMM's maternalist discourse and activism.[8]

DiQuinzio's and Hayden's efforts to unravel the meaning and impact of motherhood in public settings are timely, particularly in the current political climate, and the Woman/Mother continuum (presented earlier in this chapter) can also contribute to that endeavor. In fact, it sheds light on the scholars' opposing stances on the efficacy of maternalism, revealing, for example, that DiQuinzio (who detailed the downside of the MMM's discourse) focused on media representations that positioned marchers toward the Woman and away from the Mother end of the continuum. The press infantilized participants by presenting them as highly emotional, a pejorative associated with the devil-term Woman that damaged maternal ethos and jeopardized their "claims to equal citizenship by undermining their . . . rational autonomy" ("Love and Reason" 233). Hayden, meanwhile, attended to the positive outcomes of the MMM's affiliation with the Mother. Protesters' repeated references to children, love, protection, nourishment, altruism, morality, self-sacrifice, strength, and nation invoked the god term, lent cultural cachet to their arguments, and supported their efforts to change legislative policies and priorities. Therefore, rather than reaching opposite and irreconcilable conclusions, DiQuinzio and Hayden simply concentrated on different aspects of the Woman/Mother continuum, in each case correctly predicting the impact of god and devil terms on the MMM's public image and political effectiveness. Although the continuum cannot *resolve* feminist debates about maternalism, it can illuminate motherhood's rhetorical construction, circulation, and consequences for women.

My own policy is to adopt a both/and approach to motherhood in public discourse, recognizing that the topos produces rich rhetorical resources capable of advancing women and their civic agendas while simultaneously reinforcing limiting stereotypes and inequitable gender relations. Maternal rhetorics sometimes have disastrous consequences for women; however, they are too widespread, too powerful, and too effective to be dismissed out of hand because of associations with essentialism, binary thinking, or gender bias. Motherhood's cultural entrenchment and familiarity are, after all, the source of its persuasive potential as well as its potential peril for women. Next, I trace the construct's development, significance, and connotations in American public discourse.

The Genesis of the Mother

Motherhood, like gender, is culturally specific and historically variable. Therefore, clarifying its emergence and evolution, particularly in relation to the United States, is necessary in order to understand its contemporary rhetorical construction and political consequences. The code of motherhood began to assume its present form between the seventeenth and nineteenth centuries when, according to Michel Foucault's *The History of Sexuality*, medical, scientific, and political developments reformulated foundational beliefs about biological sex and human sexuality. As a result, new "gender fictions" of masculinity and femininity emerged that profoundly changed the meaning of motherhood, in part, by framing maternal instinct, domesticity, sexual disinterest, empathy, morality, and self-sacrifice as "natural" female characteristics. Over the course of this period, the constructs of Woman and Mother took their current shapes, resulting in a rhetorical continuum (detailed earlier in this chapter) that, I argue, continues to undergird public discourse. In this section, I detail the recent genesis of the code of motherhood, attending, in particular, to modified notions of biological sex, sexual desire, the mother/child relationship, sensibility (or empathy), and space.

Biological Sex: According to Thomas Laqueur, Emily Martin, and other historians of the body, a scientific paradigm shift transpired during the seventeenth and eighteenth centuries that revolutionized previous understandings of biological sex and gender. Prior to that time, a *one-sex model* of the human body generally prevailed, holding that men and women had identical but differently placed genitals (Laqueur 4). Male and female reproductive organs were thought to be structurally and functionally analogous—the penis corresponding to the vagina, the testes to the ovaries, and so on—with men's located outside and women's inside the body. Men and women were, therefore, thought to be "hierarchically, vertically, ordered versions of one sex," their genital variations interpreted as differences of degree rather than of kind (10). However, a series of epistemological, social, scientific, and political changes gradually displaced the model of a single sex and promoted instead one consisting of "two stable, incommensurable, opposite[s]" (6). Internal and external genitalia became markers of two distinct and profoundly different sexes.

The *two-sex model* also linked gender to the biological body, so women's reproductive capacity became the source of such defining "feminine" characteristics as maternal instinct, timidity, domesticity, and so on. Men and women's presumed sexual and gender differences coalesced into a causal or foundational force that regulated human identity, behavior, and society. Foucault speculates, in *The History of Sexuality*, that unified masculine and feminine gender ideals emerged at this point in history, displacing previously contradictory and ambiguous ideas about men's and women's fundamental character. According to Laqueur, these gender ideals supported the emergence of a heterosexual matrix that framed sexual pursuit of the opposite sex as *the* primordial, paramount human motive. Consequently, reproduction became women's biological and psychological destiny and motherhood the apex of feminine achievement, a cultural mandate that privileged the Mother over the Woman.[9]

Sexual Desire: The ascendance of the two-sex model and heterosexual matrix also produced new perceptions of sexuality, another development with a pronounced impact on the code of motherhood. Under the one-sex model, both men and women were thought to contribute to conception, which resulted "from a union of male and female seed or substances 'jointly ejaculated at mutual orgasm'" (Kipp 47). Indeed, belief in women's equal participation and pleasure during procreation was readily apparent in William Harvey's seventeenth-century description of the sexual act as "the male and the female dissolv[ing] in one voluptuous sensation" (294). A similar account appeared in *Aristotle's Masterpiece: The Secrets of Nature Displayed*, a text that had virtually nothing to do with Aristotle, by the way. This anonymous, quasi-pornographic explanation of sex, sexuality, and pregnancy was published in 1680 and circulated clandestinely throughout Britain and the United States for centuries. In poetic meter, it detailed men and women's "Instruments of Generation," noting that "Each part is fitted for the use design'd":

> The purest blood, we find, if well we heed,
> Is in the testicles turn'd into seed.
> Which by most proper channels is transmitted
> Into the place by Nature for it fitted;
> With highest sense of pleasure to excite
> In amorous combatants the more delight.
> For Nature does in this work design
> Profit and pleasure in one act to join.
> > "A Particular," n.p.

With the unsettling of the one-sex model, however, ideas about women's role in and enjoyment of procreative sex changed. As male and female genitalia became anatomically distinct sexual markers (rather than variations of a single sex), men assumed the role of active agents and women the role of passive receptacles during conception. The two-sex model posited men's pleasure (and seed) as integral and women's orgasm as irrelevant to procreation, a new perception of desire reflected in Dr. William Acton's *The Functions and Disorders of the Reproductive Organs* (1857): "As a general rule, a modest woman seldom desires any sexual gratification for herself. She submits to her husband, but only to please him and, but for the desire of maternity, would far rather be relieved from his attentions" (213). By the nineteenth century, sexual desire was coded as masculine and sexual disinterest as feminine. The new "gender fictions" discouraged women's sexual expression—whether in terms of curiosity, eagerness, or pleasure—and intercourse for duty or reproduction's sake became an attribute of the Mother.

The Mother/Child Relationship: The period also witnessed a major reformulation of relations between mothers and children. An influential expression of changing expectations was Jean-Jacques Rousseau's *Emile; or, Treatise on Education* (1762), which depicted childhood as "a special and valued period of life" and children as "innocent beings in need of prolonged protection and care." Women's "innate" maternal qualities—their natural propensities to "self-sacrifice, moral purity and narrowness of intellect"—particularly suited them for the task (E. Glenn 14). *Emile* placed mothers at the center of society, their bodies making new life possible; their care shaping children's "sentiments, habits, passions, and bodily constitution"; their instruction preparing future male citizens' "exercises of will, reason, and social participation" (Kukla 41).[10] Mothers would, therefore, determine the caliber of a nation's citizenry and health, a civic function that linked women to the polis and afforded them some measure of authority. These perceptions would become important components of the developing code of motherhood.

Sensibility: The transition to a two-sex model and emergence of new gender ideals also led to women's association with sensibility (sympathy or empathy), the capacity to connect fully with other human beings on an emotional, heart level. This quality obsessed eighteenth-century writers and philosophers, who saw the maternal body as the source of sensibility and pregnancy/breastfeeding as symbols of a requisite breakdown of boundaries between self and other: "Lauding the naturally sympathetic dispositions of women as an intrinsic component of their destined roles as mothers, numerous writers of the period referenced the connection between mother and child . . . to substantiate the claim that moral sentiments were grounded in natural laws" (Kipp 26). Feminine characteristics came to include both maternal instinct (the biological imperative to breed) and sensibility (the biological compulsion to connect), attributes that eventually transitioned into women's moral superiority to men. By the nineteenth century, the wife and mother was responsible not only for forming her children but also for reforming her husband through her exemplary love, goodness, selflessness, altruism, spirituality, and empathy—qualities that were ultimately coded as maternal.

Space: The two-sex model also contributed to the gendering of space as women's presumed interest in and aptitude for child rearing complemented the prevailing "public/male, private/female split" (Kaplan 21). The division of space into distinct gendered realms was further reinforced by the rise of industrialization in the late eighteenth and early nineteenth centuries, a period when manufacturing moved from the home to the workplace and middle- and upper-class women were recast from producers to consumers of goods. Capitalism thus exerted its own imprint on motherhood, reifying a "natural division of labor" where men ruled "the 'public' sphere of economy and polity" and women inherited "the shrunken 'private' sphere of the household" (E. Glenn 14). Privileged women were confined to tending the home and raising children, their "inactivity" a sign of social status and proper feminine comportment (Bassin, Honey, and Kaplan 45). Spatial segregation was also buttressed by the nineteenth-century *cult of true womanhood*, gendered assumptions holding that women's purity, piety, domesticity, and submissiveness inclined them toward social seclusion (Welter 152). Motherhood became firmly associated with the private sphere, and women's departures from it, especially to address civic or political topics in "masculine" public spaces, were perceived as violations of the gender code.[11]

As this brief history of motherhood suggests, the emergence of a two-sex model revised foundational notions of biological sex and gender, sexual desire, the mother/child relationship, sensibility, and space, developments that collectively reconfigured cultural beliefs about women's destiny, character, and worth. By the nineteenth century, motherhood had become the pinnacle of feminine accomplishment: The mother stood at the apex and was followed (in terms of significance) by the maiden, eagerly awaiting marriage and family; the mother and maiden were, in turn, trailed by the spinster, a pitiful figure lacking the home, husband, and children required for social consequence. These gendered perspectives, values, and expectations were ensconced within the code of motherhood and encouraged the Mother's ascendance to a god term. The code dictated that all women should crave motherhood and become mothers; those who failed to desire maternity, to become mothers, or to "manifest the qualities required by mothering" were regarded as "deviant or deficient" (DiQuinzio, *Impossibility* xiii). They joined others who likewise strayed from the code—by exhibiting sexual interest or pleasure, by pursuing their own ambitions, by focusing on a career, by entering the public sphere—and came to inhabit the devalued position of Woman, the antithesis of the Mother. These categories became lodestars of the Woman/Mother continuum and encoded the positive and negative associations integral to rhetorics of motherhood.

The Code in Daily Life

To this point, I have discussed motherhood as a part of the discursive formation of gender, as a cultural code, as a rhetorical god term, and as a historical construct. However, there is often a gap or disjunction between abstract ideas about motherhood and women's maternal experiences and practices in daily life. In this section, I explore some of the code's institutional, social, and rhetorical ramifications for women, first, by noting the impact of intersectionality on motherhood and the code's erasure of intersectional difference; second, by tracing the impact of that erasure on ethos; and third, by considering the code's influence on women's discursive production and delivery.

To begin, how does intersectionality shape motherhood? Gender is a system that marginalizes all women, but its effects are compounded by additional systems of oppression, including race, class, age, sexual orientation, disability, and so on. In most women's lives, multiple systems "overlap and cross over each other, creating complex intersections at which two, or three or more of these . . . meet" (Working Group, n.p.). Women's particular social locations and identities, then, have a profound impact on maternal experiences, practices, and expectations. Consider, for instance, the code of motherhood's uneven application across the confluences of race, ethnicity, and class. Since the nineteenth century, the code has encouraged elite white women to sequester themselves in the private sphere and devote themselves entirely to husband, home, and children while women who were working-class, poor, or of color were neither expected "to be full-time mothers" nor allowed to "harbor the illusion of a protected private haven" (E. Glenn 5). Because economic provision was "an expected part of mothering" for the latter, they instead "move[d] back and forth constantly between 'public' and 'private' labor," in the process developing distinct maternal practices that enabled them to accommodate both work and children. Patricia Hill Collins observes that African-American mothers have served not only as *bloodmothers* to their offspring and *othermothers* to their kin's and neighbors' children but also as *community othermothers* to the larger black collective (*Black Feminist Thought* 189–92). The sense of responsibility accompanying these roles—particularly the community othermother's efforts to ensure "group survival, empowerment, and identity" (P. Collins, "Shifting" 58–59)—prompted many educated nineteenth- and twentieth-century black women to become politically active and enter the public sphere, civic involvement that ran counter to mothers' conventional relegation to home and children (see Giddings; Higginbotham; Logan). African-American mothers' intersectional positioning, then, produced maternal practices, roles, and objectives that varied significantly from those promoted by the code of motherhood.

Intersectional differences, however, are often ignored within legal, educational, religious, media, and medical domains that collectively generate policies and procedures that govern women's bodies and offspring. Such organizations produce what Adrienne Rich calls the *institution of motherhood*, which works to ensure that women's potential relationships to their "powers of reproduction and to children . . . remain under male control" (13).[12] The institution of motherhood is aligned with the dominant system of gender and, therefore, frequently disregards women who are not positioned within the mainstream. This is apparent, for example, in the tensions that persist between the terms *lesbian* and *mother*, tensions produced by cultural logics holding that mothers are heterosexual and that lesbians (due to their sexual orientation) are, consequently, "non-procreative" and non-mothers (Thompson 6). The term *mother* also "reads awkwardly" against *lesbian* because the latter suggests "explicit and perverse sexuality" to many, and sexuality is emphatically *not* an attribute of the Mother (6). As a result, lesbian mothers regularly encounter suspicion, ambivalence, and discrimination in their dealings with the institution of motherhood, and something as "simple" as establishing maternity can be vexed and complicated. Similar institutional barriers confront mothers who likewise depart from convention, say by being under- or over-aged, by having disabilities, or by struggling with addictions.

Motherhood, then, is coded in ways that disregard intersectional differences, create institutional impediments for nontraditional women, and produce serious rhetorical consequences. Within public discourse, the code's promotion of broad cultural ideals and gender stereotypes tends to subsume the specificity and uniqueness of groups and individuals. Think of Michelle Obama's self-designation as "First Mom" or "Mom-in-Chief" and the way those monikers have overshadowed her impressive educational, legal, and administrative accomplishments prior to entering the White House. It is unsettling, in fact, to witness how the Mother has flattened an "incredibly smart, loquacious lioness of a woman," as eminent African-American scholar Paula Giddings aptly describes the First Lady (qtd. in Traister 49). The code of motherhood, however, may be invoked strategically for precisely this purpose as it enables rhetors to mask or minimize potentially alienating backgrounds, characteristics, or beliefs. In Obama's case, highlighting motherhood (rather than educational or professional achievements) not only distances her from another accomplished but controversial First Lady, Hillary Rodham Clinton, but also deemphasizes the potentially divisive issue of race. As rhetorically savvy as her newfound maternal ethos may be, Obama's guise as "Mom-in-Chief," nevertheless, appears tame, conventional, and stunted when compared to the charismatic, "complicated, outspoken, querulous and ambitious woman" in evidence before her husband's election (Traister 292). Such diminishment is the cost of enveloping oneself with the cloak of maternity.

Another way in which motherhood shapes women's daily lives concerns their rhetorical careers and practices. As I detail in *Regendering Delivery: The Fifth Canon and Antebellum Women Rhetors*, bearing and raising children frequently has an adverse impact on women's public involvement, routinely ending, interrupting, or deferring their persuasive endeavors.[13] Maternal rhetors must find ways of negotiating conflicting domestic and civic obligations; to do so, they have often turned to collaboration, a cooperative arrangement involving two or more people that results in a rhetorical product, performance, or event (134). Although antebellum women collaborated in order to create and deliver rhetorical texts, their cooperative practices also helped them to accommodate the code of motherhood. Maternal rhetors who stepped onto public platforms violated gender precepts that relegated them to the domestic sphere; their supportive collaborations with family, friends, servants, and supporters enabled them to fulfill private obligations and the ideals of true womanhood. Contemporary women's continuing reliance on collaboration demonstrates the method's effectiveness in reconciling motherhood with public, political engagement.

The code of motherhood, then, has a profound impact on women's experience, ethos, and rhetorical practice. In institutional terms, it erases intersectional difference and creates impediments for women whose social locations and identities depart from the norm. In persuasive terms, it tends to flatten what is individual, idiosyncratic, or distinct and to promote, instead, a familiar and nonthreatening maternal stereotype. In other words, the code subsumes specificity and substitutes the Mother, a move that can result in cruel displacement, erasing what should be admired and remembered; such displacement, however, may sometimes be a desirable outcome, so the Mother's flattening effect may be consciously selected in light of the rhetorical situation. Finally, in practical terms, the code shapes women's career patterns and encourages collaborative methods of discursive production and ideological accommodation. In each of these ways, motherhood exerts pressure on women and their lives.

Motherhood provides rhetors with persuasive means that not only reflect dominant cultural systems and gender codes but also have the potential to reify, resist, and revise them. Maternal rhetorics, then, may be used to promote conservative, progressive, or feminist ends, a capacity that is important to remember in light of critiques holding that they invariably perpetuate the status quo. Granted, maternal rhetorics *do* employ traditional assumptions about women—for example, that they are more concerned with home and children than with the polis and politics—but those assumptions can be remarkably effective at certain times, in certain places, with certain audiences. Given the code's cultural capital, women rhetors may choose to invoke it strategically in order to present themselves as mothers or make their discourse moving, memorable, and persuasive. Such use—Georgia Warnke observes in "Race, Gender, and Antiessentialist Politics"—requires women to harness the "inconsistencies" of essentialized identity and direct them "against the forms of power that impose that identity" (103). Gender categories, she argues, are not inherently or inevitably problematic; they only become so when subjects' full dimensions are denied or opportunities constrained due to a monolithic social construct (108). To apply Warnke's insights to the topic at hand, motherhood taps into a cultural code and generates rhetorical resources that are useful for forwarding change; at the same time, it also has the potential to diminish women's complexity, dimensions, and opportunities. Rhetors attuned to both the promise and peril of maternal rhetorics can employ them carefully, wisely, and well in order to protect and advance women's standing.

In coming chapters, I employ a feminist lens to investigate the terms, processes, and effects of motherhood in public discourse, exploring its beneficial and detrimental outcomes for women and identifying possibilities for change. Motherhood, after all, is formed through reciprocal movements between the experiential and the discursive plane, its transmutations from flesh and action into sign and connotation offering opportunities for reshaping social institutions and cultural codes. This back-and-forth affords women agency and makes transformation possible. Inequitable systems and codes, then, may be modified even if they cannot be entirely eradicated. Krista Ratcliffe observes that human beings are "born into language" and never "escape the dominant discourse of the symbolic"; consequently, there is no space "in which feminists may stand to begin totally anew." However, dominant discourse is not static, so there are always opportunities to revise it (Anglo-American 5). I envision such modification as incremental rather than revolutionary, as enacted piecemeal from within rather than imposed from without. I would, therefore, respectfully unsettle Audre Lorde's assertion that the master's tools will never dismantle the master's house, first, by recognizing that motherhood often serves as one of his tools and, then, by claiming its potential to reformulate his home. Tools may be used to build and reinforce as well as to dismantle and tear down. Identifying who has rhetorical recourse to motherhood, how maternal appeals are crafted, what they communicate about gender, and when they serve or subvert women's interests is arguably the first phase of the renovation project. Even as this preliminary work is underway, the next stage can begin—appropriating rhetorics of motherhood in order to disrupt and transmute the oppressive systems of gender, knowledge, and power that comprise the master's house.

2

From "Wild Woman Writer" to "Mother of Two":
Margaret Sanger, Birth Control, and Ethos Repair

Wild Woman Writer in Federal Court.
—*Richmond Virginian*, 26 August 1914

Woman Editor Writes on Sex, Is Indicted.
—*New York Evening Journal*, 25 August 1914

Woman Editor of Free Love "Bomb" Magazine in Court.
Advocates Assassination, Dynamite and Scientific Decreasing
of Birth Rate.
—*Detroit Free Press*, 26 August 1914

Mrs. Margaret H. Sanger Arraigned on Charge of Advocating
Assassination. Defends Unmarried Motherhood and Owns
"No Gods or Masters."
—*Baltimore Star*, 20 August 1914

"Advanced Ideas" of Woman Editor Meet Disapproval. Government Charges Margaret H. Sanger with Expounding Assassination and Right to Destroy.
—*Philadelphia Public Ledger*, 27 August 1914

Mrs. Sanger to Defy U.S.: Urges Birth Control.
—*New York American*, 27 August 1914

Margaret Sanger had a serious image problem in 1914. In March of that year, she founded the *Woman Rebel*, a militant, feminist paper with the masthead "No Gods, No Masters." It appeared at a time when "American radicalism was at one of its peaks of strength and breadth" (Gordon, *Woman's Body* 207). Sanger, as an editor with "advanced ideas," addressed a wide range of issues pertinent to working-class women: "I believe that woman is enslaved by the world machine, by sex convictions, by motherhood, and its present necessary childrearing, by wage-slavery, by middle-class morality, by customs, laws, and super-stitions" (Publisher's note, 1). It was also the first publication to print the term *birth control*, a subject Sanger was determined to discuss following her experience as a maternity nurse in the crowded tenements of New York's Lower East Side. There she encountered impoverished immigrants, struggling to survive in "conditions that made the so-called sacredness of motherhood a term of unspeakable irony":

> Pregnant women—drunken husbands—hungry children, children born to a heritage of disease, filth, crime—this was the order of the day. As one pregnancy followed another, a family sank deeper into the mire. And always denied contraceptive knowledge by their doctors, these women were driven to other means. On Saturday evenings before the office of a cheap abortionist they lined up, each waiting her turn. (qtd. in Reed 14)

Although her patients pleaded for birth control, the only methods avail-able to them were abstinence, *coitus interruptus*, or condoms, none of them completely in women's control and, therefore, "utterly insufficient and untrustworthy" (Katz 17.) Furthermore, even if she knew of alter-nate means of contraception, Sanger could not divulge that information unless she was willing to defy the Comstock laws. Congress passed the "broad but vaguely defined federal statute" in 1873 and prohibited use of the public mail system to transport "obscene" material, which in-cluded "every article, instrument, substance, drug, medicine, or thing" that might be used to prevent conception or produce abortion (Chesler 67–68). Eventually, the federal Comstock law "spawned a legion of state imitators," muzzling the discussion and prescription of birth control, even by medical professionals (Hull and Hoffer 36).

Sanger's inability to help her clients prompted her to research contra-ceptive methods in libraries across the country and to publish sex-edu-cation articles in leftist newspapers, including the *Call, Il Proletario,* and *Solidarity* (Reed 14). In 1912, she began a regular column, "What Every Girl Should Know," that provided women with clear, accurate, accessi-ble information about human physiology and the healthful aspects of sex.[1] Her 9 February 1913 entry on venereal disease was censored by the Post Office (which monitored mailed materials for evidence of obscen-ity), marking Sanger's first entanglement with the Comstock laws and preparing her for a similar response to the *Woman Rebel*, which was immediately suppressed by postal authorities. By August 1914, she faced grand jury indictments on three counts for publishing obscenities, each carrying a potential fine of $5,000 and jail term of ten years (Reed 30). The indictments garnered national attention, but as the chapter's opening headlines indicate, newspapers' depictions of Sanger were more likely to repel than to attract any but the most radical supporters. Their references to the editor's "advanced" ideas regarding assassination, dynamite, free love, bombs, and birth control reflected her commitment to revolutionary change on multiple fronts and alignment with socialist tenets that framed women's free sexual expression and reproductive control as by-products, not central objectives, of the larger class struggle.

However, Sanger's focus and priorities began to change after she opted to flee the country in late 1914 rather than stand trial on *Woman Rebel* charges.[2] Her year in exile proved a life-altering experience, prompting her to devote herself to the single issue of birth control and to revise her approach to its advocacy and promotion. Through contact with leading intellectuals and Neo-Malthusian groups in Britain and Europe, she encountered compelling scientific and academic arguments for contraception that promised to make it widely appealing by appeasing both "medical opponents of legalized birth control" and "middle-class fears of social unrest and race decline" (Katz 94). As Sanger observed medical efforts to promote contraception in England, Wales, Holland, France, and Spain, her goals moved from simply disseminating information to providing women with professional care and counseling in clinical settings (see Sanger, *Margaret* 125–78). By the trip's conclusion, the activist relinquished all other radical concerns and dedicated herself to creating a broad-based movement for birth control in the United States.

Therefore, following her return to America in 1915, Sanger sought the support of middle- and upper-class women as well as the attention of the press and tried to undo negative perceptions of her and her cause. Essential to these efforts was her public transformation from a "wild woman writer" to a "mother of two" who advocated birth control, a makeover made possible by her rhetorical appropriation of motherhood. Sanger harnessed its positive cultural connotations to repair ethical damage resulting from the *Woman Rebel* charges and her flight from prosecution. She also aligned contraception with motherhood, transforming its radical, immoral associations into righteous, respectable ones. Finally, the topos afforded her persuasive means for encouraging women's affiliation, for creating exigency for birth control, and for advocating changes to its legal, medical, and social status. Rooting ethos, arguments, and identification in motherhood enabled

Sanger to reposition herself and her cause from "the radical margins to mainstream respectability" (Katz xxiii). This chapter, then, focuses on the benefits that may befall women who employ maternal appeals effectively in public discourse. I examine a pivotal time in Sanger's early career—1914 through 1917—and trace how her rhetorical deployment of motherhood enabled her to repair damaged ethos, establish a strong base of support among mothers, and interject birth-control discourse into the dominant public sphere.

Reformulating ethos was key to accomplishing these objectives. Aristotle, of course, recognized ethos as one of the three artistic appeals, its particular province being the speaker's construction of character, and identified its component parts as "practical wisdom (*phronēsis*)," "virtue (*aretē*)," and "good will (*eunoia*)" (2.1.5). Displaying good ethos is especially important for rhetors who promote unconventional commitments (such as women's control over reproduction). They must make themselves and their agendas credible and virtuous if they hope to influence minds and change society. For such speakers, Carolyn Skinner observes, cultivating an audience is a crucial element of ethos construction: "Because an effective *ethos* is one that demonstrates that the rhetor's character matches the audience's values, shaping the audience and its values can contribute to a positive perception of the rhetor" ("'She Will Have Science'" 255). A speaker advocating a controversial topic like birth control, then, must "convince audience members that they are more like her (or at least potentially like her) than they originally believed," a perception she can encourage by showing that they hold beliefs and goals in common.

Motherhood provided Sanger with a set of shared precepts that enabled her to promote feminist objectives in an accessible, attractive, and nonthreatening manner and persuade women to embrace novel ideas about reproductive self-determination. It not only generated means for displaying good will, good sense, and good moral character but also provided a site where the rhetor and audience could unite conceptually, ideologically, and emotionally. Sanger presented herself as a mother and motherhood as an ideal prized by all, establishing grounds of identification for women across class lines. She focused attention, in particular, on systemic inequities related to the Comstock laws that prevented women from controlling reproduction and being the mothers they aspired to be. In this way, Sanger encouraged them to unite and take collective action to challenge legal statutes prohibiting birth control.

Aligning birth control with motherhood, however, foregrounded the interests of some women but elided others. Sanger often depicted the prototypical contraceptive user as a white, married mother with a primary focus on home and children, a representation that ignored the distinct conditions and needs of immigrant women, women of color, and unmarried women. Such exclusions, of course, validate well-known critiques by Audre Lorde, Patricia Hill Collins, bell hooks, Kimberlé Crenshaw, and Krista Ratcliffe, among others, regarding white feminism's blindness to intersectional differences stemming from ethnicity, race, class, sexual orientation, (dis)ability, and so on. Sanger has been accused of abandoning a comprehensive commitment to the reproductive rights of *all* women and advancing those of privileged white women. Such charges, to be explored more fully in coming pages, have some validity when considered in light of Sanger's fifty-year career; however, they disregard complexities and constraints inherent to the historical context and rhetorical situation that confronted the activist between 1914 and 1917, the period that witnessed the launching of a mass movement for birth control in the United States. To explain this point, I, first, examine Sanger's construction of ethos during the Progressive era; second, conduct a close reading of one of her first visual experiments with maternal ethos; and, third, trace her leveraging of motherhood to create identification and a groundswell of support for revising antiquated laws that obstructed women's access to contraception.

Crafting Ethos in the Progressive Era

Rhetorical scholars have considered the influence of setting, social location, topic, and genre on ethos formation. I review their work in this section and interweave discussion of Progressive-era discourses and concerns that informed Sanger's repair and reformulation of ethos, focusing, in particular, on maternalism, immigration, and eugenics.

In his introduction to *The Ethos of Rhetoric*, Michael Hyde explores the relationship between character and context. Tracing the etymology of the term *ethos*, he uncovers an early, "primordial" meaning that denotes "dwelling places" where people "deliberate about and 'know together' (*con-scientia*) some matter of interest. Such dwelling places define the grounds, the abodes or habitats, where a person's ethics and moral character take form and develop" (xiii). Hyde's spatial metaphor expands ethos from an artful crafting of character "that *takes place* in the orator's specific text" to one that *takes place* in the orator's specific "dwelling place" or context; ethos, then, is created in relation to "past social, political, and rhetorical transactions that inform the orator's and [the] audience's ongoing communal existence" (xvi). Michael Halloran also emphasizes the term's spatial dimensions. He envisions ethos as emerging from "habitual," public "gathering places" where people share "experiences and ideas": "To have *ethos* is to manifest the virtues most valued by the culture to and for which one speaks—in Athens: justice, courage, temperance, magnificence, magnanimity, liberality, gentleness, prudence, wisdom" (60). If we shift locations from an Athenian to an American gathering place during the Progressive era, the most exalted virtues available to women clustered around motherhood, as constituted in a powerful cultural code and its rhetorical manifestation, the god-term Mother. Indeed, sensitivity to gendered scripts, codes, and values of the period illuminates Sanger's strategic invocation of the Mother to create maternal ethos, which enabled the former woman rebel to appear seemly, sensible, and honorable; to appeal to mothers and incite them to action; and to challenge the gendered status quo in a relatively nonthreatening manner.

Part of Sanger's ethical (re)construction entailed integrating a well-established discourse into her rhetorical arsenal, maternalism. Prevalent from the late nineteenth to the early twentieth century, maternalist rhetoric typically "accepted, even idealized, women's traditional role as wife and mother but at the same time insisted that women had a duty to extend their female skills and concerns beyond their own home," thus providing women "both a motivation and a means" for justifying their public endeavors (Clapp 3–4). In many ways, maternalism was the offspring of two earlier gender ideals—republican motherhood and the cult of true womanhood. Republican motherhood emerged after the War of Independence and profoundly revised American women's social and familial roles. The fledgling nation's decision to maintain no standing army or national church (institutions that traditionally instilled discipline and morality in the populace) shifted responsibility for inculcating republican virtue to the nuclear family (Conway 4). That obligation fell chiefly to mothers, who were tasked with developing the character of American children and, thus, became "custodian[s] of civic morality" (Kerber, *Women* 11). The instructional mandate inherent to republican motherhood enabled women to argue convincingly for an extended and more rigorous education, one that would prepare them to raise informed, virtuous, patriotic sons and ensure the nation's continuing vitality.

Republican motherhood developed in tandem with a gendering of space that assigned women the domestic, private circle and men the public, political, and professional realm.[3] Over the course of the nineteenth century, middle- and upper-class women's relegation to home and hearth was reinforced by the emergent cult of true womanhood, which described feminine character as inherently pious, pure, submissive, and, of course, domestic (Welter 154). Antebellum women appropriated cultural assumptions regarding feminine purity and piety to justify their involvement in benevolent or reform associations and efforts to redress social inequality, often within the masculine public sphere (see Ginzberg; DuBois, *Feminism and Suffrage*). Maternalism, in turn, developed during the postbellum period and combined elements of republican motherhood with the cult of true womanhood, employing women's inherent domesticity, goodness, patriotism, and maternal instinct as planks to legitimate civic participation. It gave women rhetorical means for extending domestic boundaries to encompass the larger community and for undertaking the challenge of social housekeeping while ostensibly upholding conventional gender roles (as opposed to directly contesting or abandoning them) (Baker 633–35, 639–40).

Once Sanger began to foreground motherhood, she incorporated maternalism and moral righteousness into her ethos in order to exonerate direct action. Her feminism, however, also prompted a departure from conventional maternalism, for she placed women's rights and well-being—not children's—at the center of her arguments for birth control. Maternalism, nevertheless, contributed greatly to the activist's ethical repair, enabling her to hide feminist ambitions beneath the mantle of motherhood and add contraception to the list of social issues deemed appropriate for Progressive women, including school governance, sanitation, inner-city poverty, suffrage, and child labor. What is more, it provided her with established lines of argument for appealing to mothers and encouraging their "clean up" of state and federal statutes restricting the free flow of birth-control information, a strategy that I examine shortly.

Sanger's appropriation of maternalist discourse illustrates, per Halloran, that communal beliefs and values (in this case, about motherhood) are central to ethos construction; so, too, is the rhetor's location within the social context. Nedra Reynolds explores this aspect of ethos, noting that rhetors craft character within settings that are rife with power differences and conflicts. Although a rhetor may be positioned near to or far from the epicenter of political authority, "ethos is not constructed on a single site" and instead consists of "multiple negotiations that go on between self and society, between writer and reader, and among overlapping discourse communities" (332). Her observations suggest that ethos is a fluid, rather than a stable or consistent, rhetorical artifact and that a speaker's shifting locations and alliances may call for changing constructions of character. Sanger inhabited multiple positions simultaneously (as a woman, nurse, wife, mother, radical, leader, and lawbreaker) and crafted ethos strategically by "mediating within and between" roles and audiences (Reynolds 333). Through such negotiations, she established authority, gained credibility, and garnered trust while addressing multiple constituencies.

The turn from one audience to another, however, sometimes resulted in contradictory stances and arguments that seriously undermined Sanger's ethos. To illustrate, the pre-exile rhetor chiefly addressed radical and working-class readers and so relied extensively on anticapitalist analysis. That approach worked well in the early 1910s, a volatile and exciting time that witnessed frequent labor strikes in manufacturing and industrial arenas, regular suffrage marches and parades, and sufficient prosocialist sentiment to produce a viable third party in American politics. Sanger immersed herself in the tumult, joining both the Socialist Party and the Industrial Workers of the World (IWW) (Gordon, *Woman's Body* 207). Understandably, a preoccupation with class and economics characterized her early work. In the pamphlet *English Methods of Birth Control* (1915), for instance, Sanger admonished proletariat women to halt childbearing "so long as there is a class war and the workers must fight for their economic emancipation. Working women should not produce children who will become slaves to feed, fight, and toil for the enemy—Capitalism" (8–9). Because woman's primary duty was to the class struggle, she belonged "on the battlefield with her class brothers" and could, therefore, not afford to be "burdened or hampered" with children. Sanger's female proletarians were competent and capable of bold and decisive action, a representation that would alter once the rhetor returned from exile and began to address more diverse audiences.

Although she never entirely relinquished radicalism, Sanger did mute anticapitalist critique in her attempts to solicit widespread support for birth control, especially once she began to court society women whose financial resources and influential connections contributed greatly to the cause. Sanger's efforts to expand her base pushed her to develop new rhetorical frameworks that appealed to women *across* the social, economic, and class spectrum. She, therefore, turned to motherhood to establish ethos and common ground for women's identification and affiliation. She also employed maternalism to urge privileged women to form nurturing relationships with their impoverished sisters, first, by providing moral, spiritual, and economic assistance; second, by demonstrating that (elite) mothers were uniquely qualified to lead "campaigns for public social provision"; and third, by giving aid directly to poor women—rather than their husbands—in order to reverse their "economic and political dependence on men" and unsettle patriarchal barriers to effective mothering (Gordon, "Putting" 65). In adapting motherhood and maternalism to her own ends, Sanger made the controversial issue of birth control palatable to conservative women and stirred them to action on behalf of those less fortunate. The approach, however, also necessitated recasting female proletarians from class warriors to helpless victims in need of rescue, modifications that reveal tensions inherent to addressing multiple audiences.

Sanger traversed difficult rhetorical terrain in her efforts to inspire a mass movement for birth control, and her ethos and arguments sometimes shifted to an astonishing degree, depending upon whether her constituency was located on the margins or near the center of power. In "Woman, Morality, and Birth Control" (1916), for instance, she praised the positive example set by privileged mothers who practiced birth control (despite its illegality)—information that was "tenaciously withheld" from too many women. Those with access to contraceptive knowledge were "free to develop, free to enjoy in its best sense, and free to advance the interests of the community" while their men legislated, led, and controlled the nation's destiny ("Woman" 9). "[M]en, women and children of this class," Sanger remarked, "do not form any part whatever in the social problems of our times. . . . All our problems are the result of over-breeding among the working class, and if morality is to mean anything at all to us, we must regard all changes which tend toward the uplift and survival of the human race as moral" (9–10). The rhetor's assertion that the upper class played no part in the turmoil of the day was a far cry from earlier depictions of heartless industrialists preying on toiling workers. Her admiring account of the elite, however, served multiple purposes, refuting suspicions that contraception inexorably led to immorality and social decay, demonstrating that having fewer children produced a higher quality of life, framing the "over-breeding" of the working class as a population-control issue, and presenting birth control as a moral solution to the problem. Although Sanger's ulterior motive remained the same, promoting the broad dissemination of contraceptive information, the reversals apparent in her representations of the proletariat and privileged classes are often astounding; they are also understandable given her efforts to attract affluent supporters and the difficulties that accompanied that effort.

Sanger's allusions to "over-breeding" and the "uplift and survival of the human race" point to affiliated controversies that touched upon birth control in the Progressive era, including immigration, birth rates, and racial supremacy. They, too, merit consideration in order to appreciate the context in which she crafted maternal ethos. Consider, first, that in 1910 nearly 41 percent of New York City's population consisted of foreign-born residents. Second, that between 1890 and 1910, the number of immigrants from northern and western Europe dropped sharply from 87 to 19 percent while those from southern and eastern Europe swelled dramatically (Adams, Keene, and McKay 47). The latter "non-WASP" newcomers were perceived as "racially different," and their high birth rates stirred fears that they would soon "overwhelm Anglo-Saxon civilized values" (Gordon, "Putting" 66). Compounding anxieties of white engulfment by "dark-skinned" foreigners was the waning fertility of Anglo-American women, whose low birth rates raised concerns about "the nation's future in general and the advisability of contraception in particular" (McCann 3). One way in which Sanger assuaged alarm over racial decline was by representing poor and privileged women alike as white, in effect erasing ethnic difference and forging a bond of shared heritage and identity (I explore this strategy shortly in her film *Birth Control*). The rhetor also employed eugenic discourse to address apprehensions about race and reproduction.

Eugenics, the scientific study of population control, was both respected and influential during the Progressive era. It provided Sanger with a purportedly "neutral" language and "objective" method for discussing the impact of race, ethnicity, economics, and health on birth rates, topics that invariably aroused strong emotions. Although many reform groups employed eugenics to advance causes ranging from workers' rights to public education, Sanger's use has come under fire and detracted substantially from her reputation. Some scholars—for example, Ellen Chesler and James Reed—have downplayed the rhetor's reliance on eugenic discourse, arguing that she used it for the sake of expediency and did not actually uphold its tenets. Others, including Carole McCann, contend that Sanger promoted an ethically responsible version of eugenics that emphasized the impact of living conditions, rather than race or genetics, on human development and capacity. Still others lambast her for using eugenics in ways that propagated racism. Linda Gordon criticizes Sanger's American Birth Control League and its journal, the *Birth Control Review*, which regularly decried the overbreeding of African Americans, immigrants, "illiterates," and the "unfit" throughout the 1920s (*Woman's Body* 283–88). She also denounces the Negro Project, a 1939 effort sponsored by the affiliated Birth Control Federation of America that targeted African-American birth rates and distributed contraceptives to poor black (but not white) communities in the South (*Woman's Body* 332–35).

Sanger did, indeed, hold that some conditions signaled the need to avoid reproduction, conditions that included chronic poverty, alcoholism, epilepsy, and physical or mental disability. Each was a standard plank in "negative" eugenic rationales for restricting birth rates in "undesirable" populations and thereby "halting the perpetuation of their genes within the human gene pool" (Franks 40). ("Positive" eugenics, on the other hand, encouraged "fit" populations to breed and perpetuate "good" genes in the human gene pool, an argument and perspective that Sanger typically avoided.) According to Angela Franks, Sanger's eugenic views were characterized by privileged bigotry, not racism, and exhibited the "self-anointed elite's rationalized disdain for supposedly inferior types of people," limiting their reproduction on that basis. If Sanger's stance was not racist per se, it was, nevertheless, "deeply prejudicial" and revealed a preoccupation with birth rates among the poor and working classes (41). Furthermore, she was a pragmatist who stressed contraception's utility for decreasing childbearing among the disenfranchised, thereby making it attractive to those committed to preserving Anglo-Saxon "numerical and cultural supremacy" (McCann 131). Eugenics, then, proved to be a mixed blessing for Sanger: On one hand, it offered her a language, framework, and set of objectives that resonated strongly with affluent white Americans but, on the other, required sacrificing the reproductive interests of women with little status or power.

To recap my examination of ethos in the Progressive era, as Sanger's goals for the birth-control movement changed between 1914 and 1917, so, too, did her construction of character and rhetoric. She tempered radical critique in order to attract and accommodate a diverse audience, continuing to address workers and leftists but embracing the middle and upper classes as well. She continued to present economic justifications for contraception but also examined its relation to race, immigration, and eugenics. In the process of expanding her base, Sanger's ethos and arguments were sometimes inconsistent, perhaps an unavoidable consequence of "mediating within and between" multiple locations and audiences (Reynolds 333). A final element that informed her ethical (re)creation during this period was genre.

Rhetorical scholars situate ethos at the juncture of "public meaning and private selves" and envision it as "emerging through the encounter between social structure and individual strategy" (Applegarth 48). The surrounding context includes an array of available genres, symbolic forms, and persuasive opportunities that enable rhetors to "adopt subject positions and access rhetorical resources to meet social and communicative ends" (44). Risa Applegarth observes that genres produce both affordances and constraints that must be navigated during ethos construction. Considering character creation "within and among genres," then, provides another interesting perspective on Sanger's ethical choices. An astute and innovative rhetor, she was willing to experiment with any form or medium likely to advance her cause and reach a potential audience. In the early years of her career, she advocated birth control in newspaper interviews and articles; in letters, pamphlets, and flyers; in journals and speeches; and in photographs, films, and books. Later, she added conferences, radio, popular magazines, and television to her repertoire.

In the remaining pages of this chapter, I examine Sanger's creation of maternal ethos in two genres designed for mass consumption and distribution—photography and film—and trace their persuasive impact. I focus on a family photograph that she released to newspapers in the month leading up to the *Woman Rebel* trial (1916), an image that accompanied press updates across the nation and played a significant role in repairing and reshaping her ethos. Newspapers, after all, played a pivotal role in daily life during the Progressive era, as their expanding readership rates suggest: "In 1880, American newspapers had a circulation of 3.1 million, a figure rising to 15.1 million in 1900, 22.4 million in 1910, 27.8 million in 1920" (Adams, Keene, and McKay 3). By 1914, twelve cities had major papers with circulations topping 100,000, and most small towns had dailies or weeklies of their own. Submitting an image for newspaper distribution was, therefore, an effective way to reach a cross section of the country and develop a comprehensive base of support. Similarly, silent film provided Sanger access to a key constituency—women. Movie houses were one of the few public gathering places that women could go unaccompanied, and they became voracious consumers of melodramas, comedies, westerns, railroad dramas, adventure serials, travelogues, social-problem pictures, labor-capital epics, and sex-education films (Enstad 164). To reach this demographic, Sanger wrote, produced, and starred in a five-reel autobiographical film, *Birth Control* (1917).

The newspaper photograph and silent film illustrate the rhetor's savvy deployment of mass media to create ethos and reach large audiences. The photographic medium confined Sanger to visual communication but offered her a rich palette, including physical proximity to her children, the family members' positions relative to each other, their facial expressions and self-fashioning (in terms of clothes, hair, and jewelry), and their gaze relative to the viewer. The comparatively new medium of film, on the other hand, added performative and linguistic options to the visual, for instance, in the interplay of title page commentary with moving images; the intercutting of long, medium, and close-up shots; the emotional force of facial expression and bodily gesture; and the transformative power of the story. Melodrama demanded clearly delineated heroes and villains, each struggling to determine an issue's outcome or a protagonist's fate, and these demands spurred Sanger's return to class critique. She related the tale of her commitment to birth control, casting herself as a courageous mother and activist; the elite as pampered, misguided, and dastardly villains; and impoverished mothers as damsels in distress, pleading for assistance and relief.[4] Despite the two genres' distinct affordances and limitations, Sanger projected maternal ethos in both and invited viewers' admiration and identification.

Sanger's construction of ethos should also be considered in light of the photograph's and film's reception. The family photograph she disseminated to newspapers in 1916 was highly attuned to the zeitgeist and resonated with readers. Alignment between the text and context helped to ensure the image's wide circulation, which contributed enormously to her reformed public image. The same cannot be said for the film *Birth Control*. Sanger seriously misjudged the climate that followed America's entry into World War I, a period that witnessed "government intimidation of leftist radical organizations and suppression of antiwar sentiment" (Katz 197). *Birth Control*'s sensitive subject matter and vehement class critique were out of step with the times. Commissioner George Bell, who controlled film licensing in New York, protested that the film fostered "hatred of the rich by the poor," suggested intercourse between unmarried persons was safe, showed a woman in childbirth, encouraged "crime by making a martyr of a deliberate breaker of the Penal Law," and praised "the hysterical enthusiasm of the birth control advocates" (*Papers on Appeal* 7–15). He, therefore, censored the film and prevented its release to the general public. Today, all that remains of *Birth Control* are a few stills and a detailed plot summary produced by the commissioner's office, a fate suggesting the dire consequences of selecting a rhetorical strategy (or ideological approach) out of synch with one's social and political setting. Although the film never reached its intended audience, *Birth Control* remains a fascinating—if little studied—text for exploring Sanger's construction of maternal ethos and persuasive efforts to attract women.[5] This overview of ethos and the Progressive era sets the stage for a close reading of Sanger's visual rhetoric, the task to which I turn next.

Picturing Maternal Ethos

Sanger's appreciation for the rhetorical potential of motherhood may well be connected to trauma that followed her return from exile. In the fall of 1915, her estranged husband, William Sanger, stood trial for distributing her birth-control pamphlet *Family Limitation* and was sentenced to prison. In consequence, she returned to U.S. soil on 6 October 1915 in order to care for her three children—Stuart, age twelve; Grant, seven; and Peggy, five—and face *Woman Rebel* charges. The family enjoyed a brief reunion until, in a terrible turn of events, the youngest contracted pneumonia and died less than a month after her mother's arrival (Katz 169). Friends, acquaintances, even strangers flooded Sanger with condolences, and her loss piqued interest in her pending trial.

Peggy's death stimulated widespread curiosity and prompted Sanger's first rhetorical experiments with motherhood, an approach that would reformulate public perceptions of her and her cause. In fact, she, her proponents, and the press publicized her bereavement throughout January 1916, the month leading up to her scheduled trial. In an appeal to "friends and comrades," published in the *Revolt* on the fifteenth, Sanger's discussion of maternal loss worked to stir empathy and motivate action. She opened the missive with news of Peggy's demise—"I returned to this country on October 6th. . . . On the sixth of November, my little daughter died of pneumonia."—and then urged her readers to send letters to judges and senators, to hold meetings, and to forward financial contributions on her behalf. Meanwhile, on the fourteenth, Irwin Granich announced the formation of a Margaret Sanger Defense League, an organization dedicated to underwriting her legal expenses and "lifting the subject of birth control from the gutter of obscenity." (*Boston Journal*). The League's public-relations objectives included revising perceptions of the defendant and contraception, and highlighting maternal sorrow was part of its strategy: "Margaret Sanger has lost one of her children through the neglect made necessary by all this litigation, and she is penniless. We want to help her because we believe her fight is in the interests of a finer and freer humanity." In attributing Peggy's death to Sanger's fight for humanity, the League elicited sympathy for her grief, admiration for her sacrifice, respect for her noble endeavors, and contributions to her defense fund. A similar reference appeared in reporter Isaac Russell's 13 January *New York Mail* article about the upcoming *Woman Rebel* trial. After announcing that Sanger would represent herself in court, the writer raised the specter of her lost child and concluded that the mourning mother "had paid a price so high that any higher payment would seem more devastating than the people would care to see inflicted." Whether written by the rhetor, her champions, or the press, Sanger was cast as a bereaved mother, rather than a radical agitator, producing an appealing figure for popular consumption (Sanger, File no. 4).[6]

Periodicals not only provided Sanger with access to a large readership but also propagated their own perceptions of the activist. In *Controlling Representations: Depictions of Women in a Mainstream Newspaper*, Kate Adams, Michael Keene, and Melanie McKay observe that coverage between 1900 and 1920 typically praised and encouraged women's conformity to ideals of true womanhood, which continued to circulate as a Foucauldian "regime of truth." The images, articles, and headlines of mainstream newspapers like the *New York Tribune* envisioned their prototypical female reader as a "white, middle-class homemaker striving each day to assure her family's happiness and create a haven of morality and safety, apart from the work-day fracas." The feminine gender norms promoted by the *Tribune* and other popular papers of the day held that one was either "a true woman or no woman at all" (8–9). Following Peggy's death, Sanger began to align her ethos with dominant gender conventions, as was apparent in a family portrait of the mother and her two sons that appeared in newspapers around the country in January 1916 (see Figure 2.1).

Figure 2.1. Family photograph of Margaret Sanger and sons Grant and Stuart (1916).

Roland Barthes's account of first- and second-order signification (denotative and connotative meaning) is useful for decoding the image's rhetorical impact. Photographs—like language—operate on two levels: denotation, concerned with who or what is depicted, and connotation, concerned with the concepts and values communicated through the representation. Visual denotation thus refers to specific people, places, and things while visual connotation involves abstractions that are not subjective but "culturally accepted inducers of ideas" ("Photographic Message" 23). In photography, important sources of connotative meaning are objects and pose. Stuart and Grant operate as objects that signal Sanger's status as a mother. Further, those familiar with her background and recent history might interject another figure into the frame, Peggy, whose absence is palpable, lending poignancy to the scene and contributing to Sanger's ethos as a grieving mother. Sanger's pose in relation to her sons encodes the centrality of the Mother: She is draped by the boys, the youngest reclining against her breast (she leans forward protectively over him), the eldest resting his head upon her shoulder. The trio's physical proximity and contact create a visual unit that conveys the children's dependence upon their mother. Sanger's stature reinforces that impression: She towers above her sons, her height enunciating her authority and signaling her responsibility for them. The mother is unquestionably the key figure in scene, the pillar of support; remove her, and the children collapse. Through these devices, the photograph signifies on two levels simultaneously, denoting a woman with two young boys while also invoking the Mother. Sanger, thus, affiliates herself with the god term and its venerated associations, including children, home, love, empathy, protection, nourishment, altruism, morality, religion, self-sacrifice, strength, reproduction, and nation. The effect is enhanced by the family's gaze into the camera, which, as Gunther Kress and Theo Van Leeuwen remark, "demands something from the viewer, demands that the viewer enter into some kind of imaginary relations" with the subjects (122). Sanger and her sons look directly into the lens, their eyes inviting, almost commanding, viewers' identification with them.

This family tableau is a significant early example of Sanger's appropriation of motherhood to repair and reformulate ethos. Her visual performance aligned well with the press's archetypal true woman, whom Adams, Keene, and McKay describe as "white, attractive, conservatively coiffed and dressed; of average weight and height; between twenty five and forty five; married or about to be; concerned with the moral instruction of her family, the righteousness of society, and the proper maintenance of her home" (19). Sanger's conventional self-presentation in the photograph would help to make her and the issue of birth control attractive, respectable, and appealing. What is more, the medium also contributed to her construction of maternal ethos. As Barthes observes in "The Photographic Message," visual images are carefully crafted, "worked on, chosen, composed, constructed, [and] treated according to professional or ideological norms"; viewers, however, often accept them as literal, not rhetorical, artifacts, interpreting them as "objective," "unmanipulated," truthful depictions of the world as it is (18–19). The genre of the family photograph lent authenticity to Sanger's ethos as a true woman, making her enactment of motherhood seem natural, self-evident, and genuine. Her rhetorical negotiations of gender and genre indicate that ethos is a "situated practice, neither fully and freely chosen nor yet thoroughly determined, but shaped through the interaction between individual rhetors and the social and material environments within which they speak" (Applegarth 49).

Fashion also played a role in Sanger's performance of gender and construction of ethos. For the shoot, she donned a dainty, lace-collared gown and piled her hair loosely atop her head, an outfit and coiffure that, again, conformed to feminine convention. These choices were strategic, as becomes apparent when her appearance in the family portrait is contrasted with alternate self-stylings of the period. Fashion, after all, either sets a woman apart from or aligns her with dominant gender norms and expectations. As Carol Mattingly observes in *Appropriate[ing] Dress: Women's Rhetorical Style in Nineteenth-Century America*, women rhetors' "visual appearance, marking gender (feminine) and intersecting with location (public and improper for women)," could either sustain or undermine "credible ethos" (5). Aware that clothes made the woman and communicated vital information about character and values to viewers, Sanger oscillated between presenting herself as a true mother or a progressive woman in early 1916. Consider, for instance, newspaper accounts of her somewhat "masculine" appearance at the repeatedly postponed *Woman Rebel* trial (see Figure 2.2). According to a *New York Evening Mail* report on 18 January, she donned "modish attire," consisting of a "close-fitting suit of black broadcloth, patent leather pumps, white spats, and an English walking hat," a look commonly associated with the New Woman, suffragists, and other rabble rousers at odds with the status quo (Sanger, File no. 4). The outfit expressed the rebellious, nonconformist side of Sanger's character.

Figure 2.2. Margaret Sanger and sister Ethel Byrne at a *Woman Rebel* hearing (1916).

Although her "modish" attire received extensive coverage and commentary in the dailies, Sanger's maternal ethos and feminine appearance resonated far more strongly with newspapers, as becomes clear when one considers the widespread circulation of the family photograph. Its popularity is apparent in a scrapbook at the Library of Congress that holds a sampling, rather than a complete catalog, of press coverage in the weeks leading up to and following the scheduled *Woman Rebel* trial (17–31 January 1916). It contains forty-nine clippings that feature the photograph of Sanger and sons from newspapers around the country, including the *Boston Evening Record, Burlington (VT) Enterprise, Johnston (PA) Democrat, Jackson (MS) Ledger, Miami Herald, Detroit Free Press, Chicago Tribune, Louisville (KY) Courier Journal, Kansas City Star, Tulsa (OK) Democrat, Ogden (UT) Examiner, Pueblo (CO) Chieftain, Helena (MT) Record, Aberdeen (WA) World,* and *San Francisco Chronicle* (Sanger, File no. 4). Additionally, although the photograph was initially disseminated in January 1916, it continued to surface for years, accompanying articles about Sanger's 1916 and 1917 lecture tours (Sanger, File no. 5) and serving as the frontispiece of her first book, *Woman and the New Race* (1920).

National circulation of the family portrait enabled Sanger to begin recasting negative public perceptions not only of her but also of her cause. Madeline Gray comments that the picture "did more to counteract the image of the shrieking woman rebel and gain the support of important people than anything she had done before" (116), and Ellen Chesler maintains that it undermined the idea that supporting birth control was "a radical or immoral act," a necessary step in revising the issue's ethos (139). Both aspects of ethical renovation unfolded in the newspaper headlines that accompanied the family photograph, which portrayed Sanger as a birth-control advocate and linked her explicitly to her sons. These moves were apparent, for example, in the *New York Press*'s "Birth Control Champion and Her Sons"; the *St. Louis Post-Dispatch*'s "Writer on Birth Control to Be Tried in U.S. Court, and Children"; and the *New York World*'s "Birth Control Writer Who Faces Trial, and Her Sons" (see Sanger, File no. 4). These headlines played a significant role in Sanger's ethical transformation from a "wild" radical to a "mother of two." They anchored viewers' interpretations and encouraged a preferred reading of the rhetor, in this case, by setting her within a respectable, maternal framework (Barthes, "Rhetoric of the Image" 38–39). Additionally, her name was connected to one specific issue rather than the panoply of revolutionary concerns (including sex, free love, unmarried motherhood, abortion, assassination, dynamite, bombs, atheism, anarchy, and contraception) with which she was associated in the August 1914 headlines that opened this chapter; a mere seventeen months later, Sanger was publicly linked only to birth control. Headlines, therefore, yoked Sanger and her cause to motherhood and helped to dissolve their prior affiliations with militancy, lawbreaking, and socialism. Comparing 1914 and 1916 headlines about Sanger's *Woman Rebel* charges, then, reveals the rhetorical acumen and cultural resonance of her initial experiments with motherhood.

There is little question that newspapers' promotion of true womanhood constituted a form of social coercion and that some women appropriated that discourse, presenting themselves as "ladies" in order to promote policy changes concerning temperance, suffrage, child labor, prostitution, *and* birth control (Adams, Keene, McKay 9–10). Sanger's successful cooptation of gender and motherhood was evident in newspaper accounts that emphasized her femininity even as they acknowledged her crusade. The *Detroit Journal* of 3 May 1916, for instance, noted approvingly that her voice was musical, not masculine; that her diction, "though marked by frank words at times," was never vulgar; and that she used "no gestures," speaking "from behind a desk and most of the time rest[ing] her hands on it, half clinched" (Sanger, File no. 5). In other words, Sanger sat, spoke, and sounded like a true woman. Her delicacy never failed to astonish spectators, as Ruth Sawyer of the *Boston Post* learned at their first meeting. The reporter confessed in a 6 August 1916 article that she had expected "a woman of the militant type, angular and domineering" but instead encountered "a little woman, dainty and effeminate, every inch a gentlewoman." After describing the "mother of two fine boys" (who wore a "simple blue taffeta, with white embroidered collar and cuffs" and "brown hair done high on her head"), Sawyer listened to her subject's views on birth control: "I gazed at Mrs. Sanger's face. Surely this was not a woman one would apply the terms of immorality of thought and obscenity of writing to" (Sanger, File no. 5). Reporters often presented the rhetor's face, form, attire, diction, and voice as evidence of true womanhood, contributing to Sanger's ethos and altering public perceptions of her.

Due to the outpouring of support generated by Sanger's appeals and the press's sympathetic coverage of the case, the state dropped all pending *Woman Rebel* charges on 18 February 1916. Prosecutors explained that "the indictment was two years old, and that Mrs. Sanger was not a disorderly person and did not make a practice of publishing such articles," a surprising assertion given her distribution of *Family Limitation* and similar pamphlets in the interim (Sanger, *Margaret* 189). In any case, she immediately put her notoriety to good use and embarked on a three-month speaking tour (April–June 1916) that included stops in Washington, D.C., Pittsburgh, Cleveland, Akron, Chicago, Detroit, Racine, Milwaukee, St. Paul, St. Louis, Denver, Los Angeles, San Francisco, Portland, Seattle, and Spokane. At its conclusion, Sanger earned a national reputation as an advocate of contraception and inspired women across the country to launch birth-control leagues (Gordon, *Woman's Body* 228; Katz 186–93). As these events suggest, her judicious use of motherhood enabled the rhetor to renovate her public image, to sanitize the issue of birth control, and to frame it in ways that resonated with diverse audiences. Now that I've established *how* Sanger constructed maternal ethos and to what effect, I turn to her rhetorical use of motherhood to create alliances.

Appealing to Mothers

In "A Message to Mothers" (1916), published shortly after the dismissal of *Woman Rebel* charges, Sanger remarked upon the enthusiastic response she had received from "the mothers of America," who inundated her with "hundreds, even thousands of letters and requests" for contraceptive information (15). (She would later compile and publish many of these epistles in *Appeals from American Mothers* [1921] and *Motherhood in Bondage* [1928].) The rhetor did not depict the writers as languishing victims, pleading for assistance, but as active agents, capable of changing society: "The women and the mothers of America, not the courts, alone have the *power* to decide the cause of Birth Control. ASSERT THAT POWER!" (15). Uniting American women and inciting them to action were critical steps in Sanger's campaign to establish a broad-based movement for birth control, and motherhood would play a central role in that endeavor.

Sanger leveraged maternal ethos to encourage mothers' identification, forge a sense of community, and call for collective effort. This section examines the rhetor's pursuit of these objectives in the silent film *Birth Control* (1917), an intriguing project that has received little attention to date. Sanger was deeply involved in the picture, writing the screenplay and portraying herself in a story that traced the evolution of her commitment to birth control. It showed her nursing impoverished mothers in dank tenements, opening a clinic to meet their contraceptive needs, and being imprisoned for that effort. Conflating real life and make believe, *Birth Control* began production shortly after Sanger established the Brownsville Clinic in a poor section of Brooklyn, a facility that the film presented as the solution to the problems it identified. The first birth-control center in America, the Brownsville Clinic opened its doors on 16 October 1916, staffed by Sanger, her sister Ethel Byrne (a registered nurse), and Fania Mindell (a bilingual receptionist) (Katz 195). In ten days, it served over four-hundred women, each of whom paid a ten-cent registration fee to consult with Sanger or Byrne and learn to use a diaphragm. Police raided and closed the clinic on 26 October and arrested the three staff members; Sanger and Byrne would both serve jail time in 1917, their ordeals generating enormous publicity that consolidated support for birth control. Throughout the Brownsville period, the rhetor was scripting and shooting *Birth Control*; motion picture cameras even captured her 7 March 1917 release from Blackwell's Island Penitentiary in hopes of incorporating it into the film (see "Mrs. Sanger to Star in Six-Reel Film," *Chicago Post*, 28 March 1917 in Sanger, File no. 6).

Sanger attempted to address women across the economic spectrum in *Birth Control* and used motherhood to establish her own credentials, to explain the relationship between uncontrolled reproduction and laws prohibiting contraception, and to demonstrate why change was imperative. To decipher her rhetorical moves, I adopt Leslie Harris's method of exploring constructions of sameness and difference as means for encouraging affiliation and spurring social action. In "Motherhood, Race, and Gender: The Rhetoric of Women's Antislavery Activism in the *Liberty Bell* Giftbooks," Harris examines writers' depiction of maternity as a "universal" experience and their promotion of a "myth of 'true motherhood,'" an amalgam of the code of motherhood and Welter's cult of true womanhood. This myth endorsed ideals of feminine character, maternity, and domesticity that were presumed to be "natural" and common to all but were, in fact, "specific to white, upper-class women" (298). Giftbook writers applied the tenets of true motherhood to free and enslaved women alike and created similarities that promoted mothers' identification across racial lines. However, they also highlighted differences between white and black mothers that stemmed from "the peculiar institution" and prevented enslaved women from being the true mothers they aspired to be. Antislavery writers' representations of sameness and difference suggested, first, that women were united by shared maternal values and experiences and, second, that white mothers were duty-bound to combat slavery on black mothers' behalf, thereby encouraging social change (295).

Harris's method is equally useful for examining Sanger's rhetorical construction of motherhood in *Birth Control* and efforts to encourage group formation and collective action. Like the giftbook writers, Sanger, too, presented motherhood as a universal experience that united women, who not only strived to love and nurture their children but also endured similar forms of oppression. The film's mothers also shared an Anglo-Saxon background, another significant similarity as I explain shortly. Unlike the giftbook writers, Sanger displaced slavery and substituted economics and class as key sources of maternal difference. In *Birth Control*, elite women's social and financial capital enabled them to circumvent legal and medical impediments to procuring contraception, allowing them to limit their offspring and to fulfill the mandates of true motherhood. (The tenets and values of true motherhood, by the way, are analogous to what I call the code of motherhood.) Poor and working-class women, meanwhile, were denied access to contraception, so they endured continuous pregnancies, bore too many children, and struggled to raise them under daunting conditions. The film suggested that once they, too, could regulate reproduction, they would become the true mothers they desired to be. Sanger, then, presented motherhood as an experience that aligned women across class lines, detailed how economic disparity impacted child spacing and mothering, and framed injustices that derived from these conditions as susceptible to change. In this manner, she created a dialectic of similarity and difference that raised awareness and invited *all* (presumably white) women to join forces and remove impediments to birth control.

The preliminary link in this chain of reasoning was forged at the film's outset, which quickly established the protagonist's maternal ethos and fierce commitment to women's reproductive self-determination. Opening titles noted wryly that anyone who helped women "evade maternity" was automatically labeled a "law-breaker": "To the aid of those mothers comes America's most recent Joan of Arc, who, for her IDEA—Birth Control—has willingly accepted persecution and imprisonment" (Sanger, *Papers on Appeal* 70). Viewers then encountered Sanger for the first time, reading demurely behind a desk. The next title card identified her as an "honored wife and loving mother" and was followed by a scene that showed her leaving home and bidding her two children goodbye (69–70). (A total of five scenes featured Sanger with her children, each interaction demonstrating maternal affection and devotion.) From the outset, the activist was visually and verbally presented as a respectable, trustworthy, middle-class woman, whose maternal experience and compassion for mothers exonerated her fight for contraception and fueled her defiance of the Comstock laws. Sanger depicted herself as a mother and mothers' advocate and deployed maternalism to assert the authority to improve society and upset the status quo when necessary.

After creating maternal ethos, Sanger sought mothers' identification through the construction of similarity and difference. The invitation was made explicit in a sequence that, first, drew parallels between the activist and a poor mother and then contrasted them both with a pampered, misguided, and presumably childless socialite, Mrs. Fakleigh, who opposed Sanger's birth-control initiatives:

> *Sub-title*: "That evening with the woman most vitally concerned in our story."
> Picture showing Mrs. Sanger returning home, met and greeted by one of her children as she comes towards the house.
>
> *Sub-title*: "The defender of public morals."
> Picture showing Mrs. Fakleigh on a chair in a room of her house fondling a dog on her lap and reading a book entitled "Three Weeks," . . . by one Eleanor Glynn [Glyn].
>
> *Sub-title*: "—and the woman she is going to suppress as a moral menace—"
> Picture showing Margaret Sanger in a room in her home reading to her two children from a book, . . . Grimm's Fairy Tales. [See Figure 2.3.]
>
> *Sub-title*: "And the woman she is trying to help—the struggling mother, typical of a vast number of civilization martyrs."
> Picture showing a woman in what appears to be a poverty-stricken home, with a small child close by, the home surrounded in squalor, and the woman is sewing. [See Figure 2.4.] (*Papers on Appeal* 79)

The short sequence compared solitary self-indulgence with engaged motherhood: Mrs. Fakleigh sat alone, petting a lapdog and diverting herself with frivolous amusements while Sanger and the struggling mother concerned themselves with children and household tasks. A preoccupation with homely matters made allies of the two characters, signaling shared maternal values and domestic commitments that superseded class, creating grounds for affiliation.

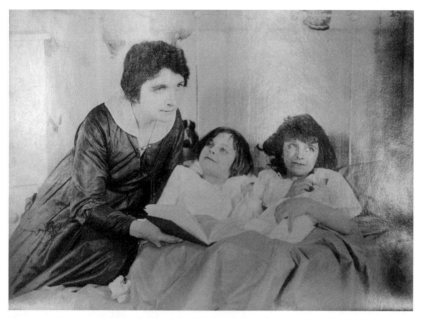

Figure 2.3. Sanger and her children (*Birth Control*, 1917).

The scene also revealed another carefully crafted similarity, whiteness. Although the issue of race/ethnicity was not addressed directly in the film, it moved like a strong current just below the surface of the text, as becomes evident when *Birth Control* is considered in relation to the waves of immigrants then reaching the nation's shores. Sanger and, more important, the impoverished mother embodied "civilized" Anglo-Saxon values, which set them apart from the eastern and southern European newcomers who were perceived (eugenically speaking) as prolifically fertile and racially degenerate (see McCann). In an attempt to sidestep xenophobic fears of racial engulfment that had the potential to undermine her arguments for birth control, Sanger depicted women on the Lower East Side as white.

The strategy becomes apparent when one examines filmic modifications to Sanger's standard conversion narrative, which detailed her life-altering encounter with Sadie Sachs, a tenement woman desperate for contraception. The rhetor first introduced Sachs—an impoverished mother suffering from a self-induced abortion (her sole option for preventing childbirth)—in the "Stump Speech" that she delivered repeatedly during her first national speaking tour (April–June 1916). While

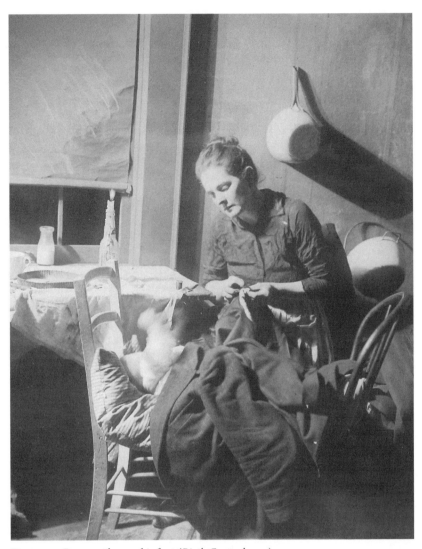

Figure 2.4. Poor mother and infant (*Birth Control*, 1917).

working as a maternity nurse, Sanger related, she experienced a classic double bind, investing weeks of intensive effort to reviving Mrs. Sachs but being prohibited from discussing the solution to her patient's predicament, birth control. Therefore, despite a full recovery, Mrs. Sachs was soon "dangerously ill" once again after being driven into the hands of a "cheap abortionist" ("Stump" 25–26). Her death left three disconsolate children, a "frantic, helpless husband," and a committed activist behind.

Recognizing the injustice of forcing women to choose between abstinence and abortion to halt unwanted pregnancies, Sanger threw away her nursing bag and vowed not to take another case until birth control was available to working-class women: "I decided I had no moral right to respect a law—a worn-out piece of parchment—obsolete in every respect, I had no right to respect this above human life, and I decided to violate it wholesale" (26–27). Mrs. Sachs's terrible plight created exigence for legalizing contraception and made Sanger's transgressions comprehensible to audiences. For these reasons, the story became a staple in Sanger's rhetorical repertoire, appearing in speeches, articles, interviews, books, and autobiographies for the rest of her life.

It also appeared in *Birth Control*. Sadie Sachs, however, was transformed into Helen Field, a name that detached the character from possible eastern European or Jewish associations and, instead, brought to mind the green meadows of England. The name change distinguished Field's racial stock from that of immigrants hailing from Hungary, Poland, Russia, or Bohemia. Sanger also took pains to emphasize the Field family's decency in the midst of "extreme squalor and poverty," presumably another attribute of its Anglo-Saxon heritage. To illustrate, the unemployed father treated his wife and five young children tenderly, offering them what little nourishment he could provide, arranging medical care for his wife with a nearby settlement house, and expressing distress at her pain (*Papers on Appeal* 71). The Fields' domesticity made them a diminished but recognizable variant of the normative white, middle-class family and signaled their respect for dominant cultural scripts. As Sadie Sachs's rechristening as Helen Field and the appearance of the woman in Figure 2.4 suggest, Sanger cast the film's impoverished mothers as WASPs.

After establishing shared racial identity, the rhetor introduced another aspiration common to all true mothers—having only as many children as could be provided for financially and emotionally. To prevent more additions to the already strapped Field family, Helen pleaded with her doctor and nurse for contraceptives: "God knows I don't want to bring any more helpless little children into this hard life" (*Papers on Appeal* 74). Her predicament demonstrated the danger of bearing more children than one's income could sustain, namely, condemning them to a deepening cycle of poverty. Each new birth meant increased deprivation for the living, a point captured in a youngster's exclamation, "Gee, Pop, every time dere's a new kid, I got ter go wit'out somethin' more!" (87). The film's object lessons underscored Sanger's belief in an "economic ethic of fertility," which held that women with the means to control reproduction would "naturally" have only as many children as their families could support (McCann 110). The desire to balance offspring and income constituted another similarity among mothers. Sanger's depiction of Helen Field's painful death due to another unwanted pregnancy was meant to stir mothers' sympathy and spawn a "movement to save others" like her (76).

Sanger identified a final element that united mothers, gender oppression. *Birth Control* portrayed men as possessing but withholding (and women as lacking but desiring) contraceptive information. Men's arrogance and misused power displaced capitalist greed as the primary source of injustice and suffering. The film's prologue, entitled "The Martyrdom of Progress," established the patriarchal origins of the fight for birth control:

> *Subtitle*: "—Under man-made regulations—as old as Society itself— Womanhood has always been a martyrdom—A supreme self-sacrifice for the greatest of all causes—the continuation of the human race."

> *Subtitle*: "Think of the mothers—all mothers—who have gone to the jaws of death that life might be created."

> *Subtitle*: "[Theirs] all the dangers, all of the anguish, all of the after-burden—but they have no voice in the matter. Man's laws say that Motherhood is her duty no matter what she may think." (*Papers on Appeal* 69–70)

After representing men as oppressors and identifying the terrible consequences of man-made law, Sanger implored women to join forces and combat patriarchal dictates that coerced reproduction. Following exile, she regularly incorporated gender inequity into her analysis, substituting the battle of the sexes for the class struggle and emphasizing women's moral superiority to men: "Man has seen fit to place the most sacred function of her body on a footing with pornography and he calls education bearing upon it as 'Filthy, vile, obscene.' Woman must undo that crime. She must raise Man's standards in this as she has done in the past to a still higher level and place the function of motherhood and its physiology where it rightly belongs" ("Notes" 3). Sanger was evidently not averse to using essentialism strategically to argue that women's biologically mandated role as mothers and moral agents qualified them to correct men, redress gendered power imbalances, and ensure women's right to reproductive self-determination (Wolff 4790). Her discourse also exhibited shades of maternalism, which authorized mothers' reform of the public, political, and legislative landscape. The rhetor, thus, presented gender oppression as another experience that gave women common cause.

In depicting women as true mothers, as WASPs, as proponents of an economic ethic of fertility, and as victims of patriarchal domination, Sanger crafted a series of similarities that allowed her to address (white) women as a group and encourage identification across class lines. However, signaling difference was equally important to her objectives, so she also spotlighted the impediments that confronted impoverished women and the disparities they produced. *Birth Control* argued that elite women's financial and social resources enabled them to circumvent the Comstock laws and obtain contraception even as working-class and impoverished women were condemned to an endless cycle of pregnancy and childbirth. Sanger traced the interrelationships among economics, birth control, and quality of life at the film's outset, contrasting a "wanted" infant—"well-formed and physically perfect, with a flower in its hand"—with an "unwanted," "ill-fed, unhealthy looking child lying upon a crib" amid "squalor and poverty." Eugenic undertones sounded in subtitles that contrasted wanted children (who were "welcomed, loved in advance, born under ideal conditions and assured of every opportunity in life") with unwanted children ("born to sick and exhausted mothers" and lacking the "stamina" needed to "meet the desperate struggle" before them) (*Papers on Appeal* 68). Sanger, thus, explored the impact of economic conditions on the material, experiential, emotional, and physical realms, which, in one case, permitted an infant to flourish and, in the other, caused it to flounder.

In another segment of the melodrama, she conducted a kind of spatial analysis in order to show the connections linking economic status, population, living conditions, and birth control. The sequence began with a newspaper reporter asking Sanger why she advocated contraception and the activist leading the reporter to a window overlooking the Lower East Side: "DOWN HERE where poverty and misfortune hold sway, Birth Control is not understood or practiced" (*Papers on Appeal* 84). The film cut to a series of "densely populated" street scenes, packed with people jostling for room on litter-strewn pavements, in the process revealing a neighborhood where "ten thousand human beings fight for bare existence in every city block!" (85). Sanger and the reporter then moved to a window on the opposite wall and examined the prosperous Upper East Side, which featured modern apartment buildings, tree-filled parks, and nannies pushing perambulators: "UP THERE—where wealth and culture reign and luxury is commonplace, Birth Control is both understood and practiced" (85). The neighborhood sustained a mere "thousand to the block," making it a "paradise for children." Sanger and the reporter continued to cross the room, noting disparities in the health of privileged and poor mothers (the latter malnourished and exhausted from repeated pregnancies), in their number of offspring, and in the quantity of resources. An uptown family, for instance, featured one "petted" child surrounded by "luxuries and advantages enough for ten children" while a downtown family hosted a "whole flock of little ones" and lacked "bare necessities" for a single child (86). Throughout her spatial rendering of the class divide, Sanger showed how financial and social capital impacted women's (in)ability to control conception: "The poor, who need Birth Control knowledge, are denied it by the laws—while the rich, able to rear families, easily purchase the information from Doctors willing to take the risk for money" (87). Uptown and downtown women's assets determined their recourse to contraceptives and safe abortions as well as their number of children. In illuminating the complex, interlocking relationships among economics, birth control, and birth rates, Sanger refuted arguments that attributed overpopulation to "the greater fecundity" or "mental inferiority" of "lesser stocks" (McCann 111). Highlighting material and social differences also suggested that the resulting disparities among mothers stemmed from conditions susceptible to change, a critical building block of Sanger's analysis.

Despite differences among women rooted in financial status, access to contraceptives, and rates of childbirth, one thing remained constant—the beating "mother heart." Leslie Harris observes that abolitionist women presented motherhood (or the "mother heart") not only as an "incredibly powerful" experience that enabled "white activists to speak 'with one voice'" but also as a platform of such "exceptional emotional" force that its impact was virtually "unstoppable" (301–2). Sanger's appeals to a common mother heart likewise encouraged (white) women's identification across class lines and inspired collective action to address circumstances that oppressed the poor. To demonstrate disadvantaged women's sincere desire to be true mothers, the rhetor depicted them sympathetically as "honest," "self-respecting" women "whose only crime [was] poverty and ill-health" (*Papers on Appeal* 86). Those conditions, however, were not sufficient to quell the maternal heart: "*Downtown*—where each new mouth adds to the killing burden and means self-denial for the others of the family, the newcomer is not so welcome, tho' afterwards it gets its full share of love" (86). Even in the midst of crushing poverty, mothers' concern for their children's well-being motivated their demand for contraception: A woman married to an abusive "drunkard" confessed "terror that the awful drink might fall on a child I'd have" (92); another, who learned of epilepsy in her husband's family, cried that it drove her "mad to think of bringing such a thing to an innocent babe" (93); a mother with an unemployed spouse explained that her children were "hungry and cold," so she wanted to avoid bringing more into the world (90). The vignettes featured caring women without means either to provide adequately for their offspring or to obtain birth control; lacking necessary resources, they were trapped in a never-ending spiral of repeated pregnancies and escalating want. Sanger's compassionate rendition of tenement women departed significantly from their usual treatment in the daily press, which showed them "living slovenly and immorally," "ruining children," and "requiring state and philanthropic assistance because of their lack of thrift and planning" (Adams, Keene, and McKay 9). Such coverage "othered" poor, immigrant, and working-class women; *Birth Control*, in contrast, presented mothers in squalid conditions with sensitivity and demonstrated the senselessness of statutes that obstructed their reproductive control.

Detailing differences in financial, medical, and social resources and their impact on women set the stage for Sanger's solution—clinics to provide *all* women with contraceptives. Such facilities would compensate for material and economic inequalities and permit more women to be good mothers. By linking women's desire for contraception to true motherhood, Sanger refuted misconceptions about birth control's immorality, a viewpoint given voice by police as they raided the clinic and called the women within "unnatural creatures—monsters who call yourselves mothers" (*Papers on Appeal* 95). In Sanger's hands, motherhood became a basis for women's affiliation across class lines and a spur to social change. As the film's central figure, she exemplified the moral, compassionate, altruistic mother, daring to do the right thing and willing to pay "the heavy penalty for flying in the face of convention" (96). The picture, thus, served both an educational purpose—teaching women about gender oppression, economics, birth rates, laws, living conditions, and contraception—and an inspirational one, with Sanger's noble actions motivating others to behave similarly. *Birth Control* ended with an image of the imprisoned, crestfallen activist, gazing forlornly through the bars of her cell while a final subtitle declared, "No matter what happens, the work shall go on" (96). It was an expression of faith that encouraged others to continue the fight for birth control until Sanger left jail and rejoined the battle.

Through its exemplary protagonist and positive characterization of mothers and mothering, *Birth Control* made a persuasive case for revising the Comstock laws. Calling for reform, rather than revolution, the film's provocative subject matter and militant discourse led to its banning. Sanger's lost film, nevertheless, illustrates her savvy rhetorical use of motherhood to encourage women's identification and collective action. She highlighted similarities as well as differences in order to show how status and statutes constrained women's management of fertility and ability to be true mothers. In developing a maternal framework for birth control, she garnered enthusiastic support from women across the economic spectrum and placed the issue on the national agenda, establishing a mass movement in the process. That paradigm, however, chiefly served the interests of privileged white women and erased those of women positioned otherwise. A closer look at the "structural leaks, seams and scaffolding" of Sanger's maternal framework is needed in order to understand not only who was "denied, hidden, or excluded" but also how and why (Chandler 82); I explore its tensions and elisions, accomplishments and consequences, next.

Aligning Birth Control with Motherhood

Motherhood became a central feature of Sanger's discourse between 1914 and 1917, enabling her to craft ethos, invite identification, highlight social injustice, and motivate women to join a burgeoning social movement. Aligning contraception with motherhood also transformed the issue in the public eye, reformulating it from a radical and immoral concern into a respectable and appealing one. Sanger's maternal framework, therefore, contributed significantly to her cause's ethical revision, a process that was apparent, for example, in newspaper coverage of the Brownsville Clinic. The facility, its clients, and the arrest, trial, and imprisonment of Sanger and Byrne produced "tremendous national publicity for the fledgling birth-control movement, spreading the debate over the legalization of contraception to households, club meetings, and union halls" (Katz 195). And much of that coverage overtly linked birth control to motherhood.

The connection surfaced repeatedly in articles that detailed the deteriorating conditions of the Brownsville neighborhood and its female residents' poverty and need for contraception. To illustrate, B. J. O'Donnell's "These Mothers Spread Birth Control Message, Defying Police Who Find Secret Clinic" featured a photograph of Sanger and four women in consultation; its caption explained that she was giving "oral information on birth control to mothers" (*Toledo News Bee*, 28 October 1916, in Sanger, File no. 7). Consistently emphasizing the maternal status of the clinic's clients, O'Donnell noted admiringly that "forbidden" instruction had been delivered to "thousands of mothers . . . in the most remarkable mouth-to-mouth campaign of sex education ever conducted in this country." The reporter also quoted neighborhood women whose determination to limit family size made them fiercely protective of Sanger: "We are too poor to pay the doctor to tell us what you have told us. If the police fight you, they must fight us too." Another article, "A Revolt against Motherhood," received a full-page spread in the *New York Herald* and focused on the first meeting of the Brownsville Mothers' Club for Birth Control, remarking that its members "had revolted, not against motherhood . . . but against the infliction of punishment on those who were trying to help them to keep from bringing into the world more children than they could care for" (4 March 1917, in Sanger, File no. 7). Departing from Sanger's tactic of minimizing immigration, race, and ethnicity (apparent in the film *Birth Control*), both articles highlighted Brownsville women's national origins and religious affiliations. O'Donnell described clinic clientele as "scrubwomen, maids—women who toil" of Russian, Polish, and Hungarian descent while "A Revolt" identified them as poor, "respectable," "clean," "neatly dressed," "Jewish" women. The coverage was generally respectful, highlighting the women's maternal standing, values, and concerns. "A Revolt" observed that club members' "kindly, self-respecting faces" revealed "maternal sweetness and that capacity which means competent, as well as devoted, motherhood." In a series of vignettes, mothers recounted moving tales about pregnancy, childbirth, abortion, miscarriage, infant death, ill health, inadequate housing, and the costs of too many children in the midst of poverty. The stories were visually reinforced by four photographs of tenement life, one showing nine people asleep in two small beds and another displaying a mother and four children doing piece work in a tiny kitchen. The overcrowding and deplorable conditions captured by the images validated the mothers' desire to restrict family size. These compassionate accounts of Brownsville women and their need for contraception suggest that Sanger's maternal framework was successfully connecting the issue to motherhood (rather than radical-ism), eliciting positive press coverage, and enhancing the propriety of birth control.

In addition to earning the appreciation of their Brooklyn clients, Sanger and her cohorts' efforts also attracted elite supporters. Prominent socialites—including Mrs. Rublee, Mrs. Pinchot, Mrs. Delafield, Mrs. Harriman, Mrs. Tiffany, and Mrs. LaFollette—formed a Committee of 100 in January 1917, its manifesto proclaiming, "We desire to help in forming a body of public opinion which will lead to the repeal of all laws, Federal and State, which make the giving out of information on the subject of Birth Control a criminal offense and which class such information with obscenity and indecency" (qtd. in Lade 117). This in-fluential group of women not only helped to defray the plaintiffs' legal expenses but also coordinated a comprehensive publicity campaign for legalizing contraception; additionally, with the financial assistance of Juliet Barrett Rublee, Sanger launched the *Birth Control Review* in early 1917, a periodical that served as the movement's official mouthpiece for decades (Katz xxxviii).[7]

The vision and bravery inherent to opening the first birth-control clinic in America drew women from both sides of the economic divide to Sanger's side, and the press foregrounded their diversity in its coverage of the Brownsville trials. At Byrne's hearing, papers noted the presence of "prominent" society women but paid special attention to Mrs. Rose Halpern, a "poorly clad" Brownsville mother of six who testified that her husband's $17 a week salary as a garment worker was insufficient for their large family and thus demonstrated the need for birth control ("Mrs. Sanger's Aid Is Found Guilty," *New York Times*, 9 January 1917, in Sanger, File no. 7). A similar cross-section of supporters appeared on Sanger's behalf, as the *Tribune* wryly observed in "Disciples of Mrs. Sanger, Rich and Poor, Watch Trial": "The East Side is the East Side and the West Side is the West Side, and seldom the twain shall meet. . . . But these two social extremes foregathered yesterday at the birth control trial of Mrs. Margaret Sanger." The spectacle of "society and club women in the front rows of seats and limousines waiting outside" lent the proceedings "the color of a reception, with Mrs. Sanger as the guest of honor"; meanwhile, the "other social extreme" waited outside the courtroom, "women of the poorer sections" who held "their babies in their arms" and left others at home in order to be there (*New York Tribune*, 30 January 1917, in Sanger, File no. 7). Women from across the city expressed their support not only through their physical presence at the courthouse but also by pinning green ribbons to their lapels "as a sign of silent protest" against Sanger's imprisonment ("Mrs. Sanger and Her Interpreter at 'Clinic' Found Guilty," *New York Herald,* 3 February 1917, in Sanger, File no. 7). As these accounts suggest, Sanger's newfound emphasis on motherhood was attracting growing numbers to her cause and prompting sympathetic news coverage.

However, even as the rhetor's maternal framework drew a wide assortment of adherents and transformed birth control into a valid, even valuable, topic of public discussion, it excluded significant numbers of women who were also vitally interested in the issue. Framing, Daniel Chandler remarks, is "always highly and unavoidably selective" (133). Within the terms of her framework, Sanger constructed a prototypical user of contraception who operated synecdochically, the part representing the whole, within her discourse. A married, middle-class, WASP mother represented *all* women, despite the fact that many were positioned otherwise by race, ethnicity, nationality, marital status, religion, economics, and so on. The danger of Sanger's maternal framework was that it appeared to tell "the whole truth" but actually presented only a limited and partial perspective. In consequence, the developing movement for birth control elided women whose lives, locations, and identities differed from Sanger's prototype, ignoring the contraceptive needs of unmarried women, the distinct family norms of other ethnic groups, and the special vulnerability of women of color.

To elaborate on these points, her maternal framework presented contraceptive users as married, not single. Situating sex within the confines of marriage enabled the rhetor to circumvent objections that birth control encouraged illicit sex and promiscuity but also meant abandoning the needs of unmarried women, a dramatic turnabout from the position she once advanced in *Woman Rebel.* Prior to exile, Sanger fiercely defended women's sexual equality, free sexual expression, and prerogative to decide when or whether to give birth in such articles as the "Right to Be an Unmarried Mother, the Right to Destroy, and the Right to Create" (Gray 72), addressing a progressive, socialist audience that accepted candid discussion of the issues. However, she muffled these convictions in order to position birth control advantageously within a dominant cultural paradigm that largely confined women's sexuality to marriage and motherhood. Although the choice made sense in light of her objectives to rehabilitate contraception's ethos and establish a comprehensive base of support, it also had some serious and negative long-term consequences. To justify legalizing birth control, Sanger increasingly emphasized *society's* need "to protect maternal and infant health," *families'* need "to limit their size to their incomes," and the *nation's* need "to control the size and ethnic character of its population," rationales that jettisoned *women's* need to "control their fertility to their own ends" (McCann 3). Relinquishing women's sexuality—whether in or out of wedlock—as sufficient grounds for birth control was one casualty of Sanger's maternal framework. In consequence, unmarried women were among the last to benefit from Sanger's challenges to the Comstock laws and efforts to decriminalize contraception. They did not win the right to practice birth control until the Supreme Court's *Eisenstadt v. Baird* decision in 1972 (Chesler 376).

Promulgating a framework that assumed mothers were white, middle-class, and married made it easy for the movement to ignore women who were situated differently. Esther Katz contends that Sanger's efforts to appeal to mainstream audiences produced "a new detachment from her previous identification with working-class women," who became "the *objects* rather than the *instigators* of reform" (96, my emphasis). Evelyn Nakano Glenn, meanwhile, holds that Sanger entered into a "kind of devil's pact" and traded away "the rights of immigrant women and women of color to *have* children [in order] to gain the rights of middle-class women to *limit* their fertility" (17–18, my emphasis). The extent to which she abandoned disempowered women is debatable, but there is no question that they subsequently struggled with multiple forms of reproductive injustice, including disproportionate rates of sterilization and use as uninformed subjects in contraceptive research (Gutiérrez 687–89). Additionally her enthusiasm for an economic ethic of fertility completely disregarded alternate cultural traditions that valued having large numbers of children (see, for example, Elena Gutiérrez on Latinas, reproduction, and nationalism). The biases of race, class, and condition inherent to the code of motherhood were, therefore, embedded within Sanger's maternal framework and subsequently incorporated into the birth-control movement itself, which discounted significant differences among women for decades.

Despite critical slippages resulting from her framework, Sanger's rhetorical appropriation of motherhood, nevertheless, enabled her to promote feminist change. In 1918, her persistent efforts to challenge and revise laws prohibiting contraception began to bear fruit: Judge Frederick Crane reviewed an appeal of the Brownsville case and ruled that doctors had the right to prescribe birth control for general health reasons, a decision that marked an important legal breakthrough and enabled Sanger to operate birth-control clinics in the state of New York, provided they were staffed by a physician (Reed 80; Katz 231). The activist subsequently worked to modify federal and other state statutes in similar fashion. Following Brownsville, she generally pursued less confrontational means of engagement and concentrated instead on establishing a variety of public forums for birth control, including journals, conferences, and research centers. Sanger, in other words, became a mainstream reformer. However, despite her adoption of more moderate tactics, she would repeatedly be arrested, banned, and blacklisted in coming years, setbacks that did not curb her productivity in the least. She established the journal *Birth Control Review* (1917); opened the Clinical Research Bureau (1923) to provide birth-control services and collect statistical data about the effectiveness of different contraceptive methods (Katz 348); organized and attended national and international conferences on birth control; conducted numerous international speaking tours, making women's reproductive control a global issue; founded the American Birth Control League (1921), a "national organization with an ambitious agenda of legislative reform, education, and research" that evolved into the Planned Parenthood Federation of America in 1942 and the International Planned Parenthood Federation in 1948 (Katz 272); and published numerous books, including *Woman and the New Race* (1920), *The Pivot of Civilization* (1922), *Happiness in Marriage* (1926), *Motherhood in Bondage* (1928), and two autobiographies (Sanger, *Margaret* 430). She also faithfully contested the Comstock laws, and contraceptives were finally removed from the roster of obscene and contraband items in 1970—four years after Sanger's death at the age of eighty-six (Reed 314).

According to Jennifer Emerling Bone, Sanger played a vital role in creating a discursive context where "she and others could argue against those . . . who worked to silence the conversation on contraception" (31). The verbal and visual rhetorics examined in this chapter trace birth control's journey from a small, socialist enclave into the dominant public sphere, a journey that was in no small measure assisted by Sanger's appropriation of motherhood. By carefully cultivating a maternal framework for her cause, she severed contraception from its radical, illegal, immoral connotations and transformed it into a serious, compelling, and respectable issue for public debate and advocacy. Motherhood also enabled the rhetor to repair and reformulate her own damaged ethos and to discover "universal" grounds for women's identification and affiliation. Finally, it contributed to her crafting of a "resilient and compelling change narrative," which Judith Stadtman Tucker observes is essential for establishing broad-based social movements (207). Engaging change narratives create "a map to a specific destination—that is, they identify a social problem and who or what is harmed by it, propose a realistic way to fix it, and provide an attractive vision of social life once the problem is removed" (Stadtman Tucker 207–8). Sanger's rhetorical embrace of motherhood gave life to the map, journey, and destination she presented to audiences. She detailed the problems created by laws prohibiting contraception and their pernicious consequences for women; she cast birth-control clinics as a solution to the identified problems; and she promised an improved quality of life following reform of the Comstock laws. Sanger's maternal ethos and appeals shrouded the feminist nature of the journey outlined on her map, for instance, by obscuring disruptions to the gendered status quo that would attend giving women power over their own fertility. There is irony, of course, to the former woman rebel employing conventional constructs of gender she once contested vehemently. In adopting a maternal framework, Sanger compromised her politics and sacrificed the reproductive interests of far too many women for far too long. Her accomplishments, however, were also substantial, contributing to the creation of a legal and social environment that recognized women's right to control their own bodies. Sadly, such environments, are fragile, susceptible to backlash and deterioration. The reproductive freedoms resulting, in part, from Sanger's maternal rhetorics have been repeatedly constricted in recent decades, making them all the more precious and worth defending. I address the erosion of women's reproductive rights more fully in chapter 4 but, first, turn to the intersections of motherhood, race, and cultural memory.

3

Motherhood, Civil Rights, and Remembrance:
Recuperating Diane Nash

Diane Nash Bevel was tried in Jackson for teaching the techniques of nonviolence to Negro youngsters; the charge was "contributing to the delinquency of minors" and she was sentenced to
two years in jail. Four months pregnant, she insisted on going to
jail rather than putting up bond, saying: "I can no longer cooperate with the evil and corrupt court system of this state. Since my
child will be a black child, born in Mississippi, whether I am in
jail or not he will be born in prison." After a short stay in prison,
she was released.

—Howard Zinn, *SNCC: The New Abolitionists*

When Diane Nash entered the Hinds County Courthouse on 31
April 1962, fully prepared to begin serving a two-year prison term,
the twenty-three-year-old leader of the Student Nonviolent Coordinating
Committee (SNCC) was protesting southern segregation and sending
a message to the broader civil-rights community. She was convinced
that the movement was relinquishing jail-no-bail policy, a coordinated
effort in which arrested protesters refused to pay fines or put up bail and,
instead, remained in prison. Nash believed that an immediate return to the
policy was imperative, first, to lighten the ruinous financial demands that
bonds placed on cash-strapped organizations like the Southern Christian
Leadership Council (SCLC) and, second, to exert moral pressure on and
direct media attention to the South, both fundamental principles of
nonviolent resistance. To ensure that her perspective and purpose were
clear to others, she detailed the problem with current practices as well
as her proposed solution in a two-paragraph press release and three-
page letter to civil-rights workers. (For full text, see the appendix.) These
documents circulated widely and reinvigorated movement discussion
about the potential of mass incarceration.

One of the press release's two paragraphs and seventeen of the letter's eighteen paragraphs detailed reasons for widespread adoption of jail-no-bail policy; each text also devoted a single paragraph to Nash's physical condition, addressing the perceived irreconcilability of pregnancy, politics, and prison:

> Some people have asked me how I can do this when I am expecting my first child in September. I have searched my soul about this and considered it in prayer. I have reached the conclusion that in the long run this will be the best thing I can do for my child. This will be a black child born in Mississippi and thus wherever he is born he will be in prison. I believe that if I go to jail now it may help hasten that day when my child and all children will be free—not only on the day of their birth but for all of their lives. ("Message" 1)

Nash employed a variety of maternal appeals to justify activating her sentence while pregnant. Arguing that immediate incarceration would serve her child's long-term interests presented readers with sound reasons for her action; mentioning soul searching, prayer, and contemplation regarding its possible consequences for her pregnancy created ethos; and declaring faith that self-sacrifice would secure black children's freedom stirred pathos. Each appeal alluded to and garnered strength from the expectant rhetor's condition (see Figure 3.1).

Although she incorporated motherhood brilliantly into the single paragraph devoted to the topic, Nash did not otherwise use maternal appeals in either the press release or letter, a decision that, in retrospect, was surely a missed rhetorical opportunity. The civil-rights activist may not have fully grasped or exploited the available means of persuasion afforded by her pregnancy, but subsequent chroniclers of the event certainly did. For decades, historians focused almost exclusively on Nash's impending motherhood, ignoring her nonviolent principles and policy objectives and reshaping the incident in troubling ways. This is apparent, for example, in Howard Zinn's epigraph, which presents a noble, idealistic mother bravely entering a racist stronghold in order to promote black children's freedom, a poignant and dramatic portrait that fails to mention the term *jail-without-bail*. Other writers followed suit, representing her as a courageous, committed, pregnant activist but overlooking her strategic and organizational contributions to civil-rights initiatives. Such depictions ultimately pushed Nash into the background of movement history.

Figure 3.1. Diane Nash, Jailbird for Freedom (1963). Wisconsin Historical Society, WHi-91968.

Motherhood, then, enabled Nash to create a stirring and unforgettable message but also cast her in a supporting role in the official record. Her relegation to the sidelines is illuminated by considering motherhood as a cultural code, rhetorical topos, god term, and social practice. The process began with the rhetor's use of the motherhood topos and crafting of appeals so compelling that they dominated subsequent accounts of the event. Historians elaborated and extended Nash's appeals, invoking the code of motherhood and creating affecting narratives that commemorated her as a Mother, rather than a strategist or leader. Furthermore, Nash's maternal and rhetorical practices also contributed to her displacement: She retired from the movement's front lines following the birth of her first child and, thereafter, collaborated with her husband—SNCC and SCLC organizer James Bevel—on major civil-rights campaigns. She frequently remained at home with their children while he supervised their projects in the field, an arrangement that garnered Bevel the glory and rendered Nash invisible. Collectively, these interwoven strands reveal how motherhood, on the one hand, generated powerful persuasive means and, on the other, compromised Nash's rightful place in cultural memory.

This chapter builds upon my examination of Margaret Sanger, whose rhetorical invocation of motherhood enabled her to push controversy (including radicalism and law breaking) into the background, to project maternal ethos, and to attract supporters to the birth-control movement. In Nash's case, motherhood, likewise, enabled her to justify her decision to enter jail while pregnant, but it also had negative ramifications that fueled her marginalization. If the Sanger chapter highlighted the potential benefits of maternity in public discourse, this one uncovers its dangers and disadvantages for women. In coming pages, I trace the impact of motherhood on Nash's legacy by examining her rhetoric and movement objectives on this occasion, by analyzing subsequent renditions of the event, and by considering the activist's maternal and rhetorical practices.

Nash as Rhetor and Strategist

As she readied herself to enter prison in 1962, Nash was already well known in civil-rights circles and well versed in jail-without-bail policy. Her involvement in the movement had begun in 1959 when, as a Fisk University sophomore, she completed James Lawson's workshop on nonviolent resistance and emerged as a leader of the Nashville sit-ins, a sprawling campaign that lasted from February to May 1960 and successfully integrated many of the city's lunch counters and public venues. Nash's first experience with jail-no-bail strategy transpired during this period. In a coordinated effort to put pressure on the justice system and heighten community awareness of racism, arrested protesters declined to pay their $50 fines and opted for jail instead, as Nash, their spokesperson, explained to the court: "We feel that if we pay these fines we would be contributing to and supporting the injustice and immoral practices that have been performed in the arrest and conviction of the defendants" (Westmoreland-White, n.p.). She helped found SNCC in April 1960 and subsequently guided many of its direct-action desegregation efforts in the South, endeavors that often led to her imprisonment. In early 1961, for example, she and three other SNCC members joined students in Rock Hill, South Carolina—where sit-ins had been ongoing for a year with little effect. In hopes of reviving the campaign, Rock Hill students agreed to change strategy and stop posting bail following arrest; Nash showed support by spending the month of February in jail alongside them (Jones, n.p.).

The activist's next major encounter with jail-no-bail policy involved the Freedom Rides. May 1961 witnessed the departure of black and white bus passengers who were determined to ride from the nation's capital to New Orleans in order to test whether interstate travel was, in fact, desegregated as federal law mandated. Their journey through the Deep South was uneventful until they reached Alabama, where mob violence led to the burning of a Freedom Bus outside Anniston and the beating of Riders in Birmingham, events that ground the endeavor to a halt (see Arsenault). Convinced that permitting violence to stop the initiative would mean the end of the civil-rights movement, Nash resuscitated the Freedom Rides despite U.S. Attorney General Robert Kennedy's pleas for a cooling-off period (Nash, "Inside" 53). She arranged for a steady stream of college-age passengers to ride interstate buses from Alabama to Jackson, Mississippi; after disembarking, they were immediately charged with breaching the peace and arrested. Nash convinced them to forgo bail and remain in jail, so between 24 May and 13 September 1961, 328 Riders filled city and county jails as well as the state's infamous Parchman Prison ("Short History," n.p.). Although the major thrust of the Freedom Rides ended in September 1961 when the Interstate Commerce Commission issued new regulations enforcing the desegregation of interstate buses and terminals, the episode demonstrated to the wider movement "that 'nonviolent direct action' and 'jail—no bail' offered a successful way forward" ("Short History," n.p.). These approaches would underpin future desegregation campaigns in Albany, Birmingham, and Selma, events that Nash also played a major role in strategizing and planning.

To oversee the Jackson leg of the Freedom Rides, Nash moved to Mississippi in the summer of 1961 with SNCC colleagues Bernard Lafayette and soon-to-be-husband James Bevel. The trio encountered such an entrenched history of racism and intimidation that they had little success recruiting adults for the Rides and so began training teenage volunteers (Halberstam 391). Soon, Nash, Bevel, and Lafayette were each charged with and convicted for contributing to the delinquency of minors, tried and sentenced in city court, and freed on bond while awaiting an appeal hearing (393).[1] When the time for the hearing arrived, however, Nash was no longer willing to cooperate with the state of Mississippi ("Dianne Nash"1, 6). Her letter to civil-rights workers explained why, detailing the absurdity of protesting segregation, undergoing arrest, bailing out of jail, and then placing matters in the hands of an "evil and corrupt court system." Protestors would not receive justice in a state where they were arrested on spurious charges (such as breaching the peace, criminal anarchy, conspiracy to violate trespass law, and corrupting minors) instead of the real issue—desegregation; were tried in segregated courtrooms; and were required to "pay the bill for this humiliation in court costs" (Nash, "Message" 2). Nash was alarmed at the "skyrocketing expense" of bailing out protesters and convinced that the practice was undermining the movement's potential: "I think we all realize what it would mean if we had hundreds and thousands of people across the South prepared to go to jail and stay. There can be no doubt that our battle would be won" (3). Leaving jail deprived the movement of its most powerful tool, "truth force and soul force." Imprisoned protesters not only put pressure on the system but also exemplified "redemption through suffering," thereby creating the possibility of real change:

> When we leave the jails under bond we lose our opportunity to witness—to prick the conscience of the oppressing group and to appeal to the imagination of the oppressed group and inspire them. . . . Gandhi said the difference between people who are recklessly breaking the law and those who are standing on a moral principle is . . . [willingness] to take the consequences of their action. When they do this a whole community, indeed a whole nation and the world, may be awakened, and the sights of all society are raised to a new level. (2)

Confident that the actions of "a few people, even one person, can move mountains," Nash was determined to do what she asked of others: "Even if we cannot honestly foresee great effects from our stand, it is my belief that each of us must act on our own conscience—do the thing we know in our hearts is right. . . . I think each of us—regardless of what others may do—must make our own decision, alone and for ourselves. I have made mine" (3). The rhetor's commitment to spiritual principle and self-sacrifice, her vision and courage, created formidable ethos and stirred strong emotion. Most of the letter, however, marshaled logical proofs to support the claim that social justice was best served by resisting a corrupt system and staying in jail. In all, fourteen of eighteen letter paragraphs detailed financial, organizational, tactical, and spiritual arguments for jail-no-bail. Reasoned analysis, then, was the rhetor's preferred method for influencing others and shaping movement action.

However, Nash could not make a compelling case without also addressing her physical condition. In halting the appeal process, she anguished over the potential consequences of resistant action for her pregnancy: "I sat out in the cotton fields and thought about my strategy for a very long time" (2008 interview). Although she did not want to serve time while expecting, give birth in jail, or risk separation from her child, Nash decided it was imperative to set an example and urge widespread adoption of jail-no-bail policy. To explain why, she devoted a paragraph to the subject in both the letter and the press release although the differing lengths of those documents affect the material's weight and significance. The press release ended with the motherhood paragraph and brought the text to a memorable conclusion. Meanwhile, the paragraph's early positioning in the letter—where it was the fourth of eighteen paragraphs—diluted its impact considerably, suggesting some discomfort with the topic. (In our 2008 interview, Nash attributed her limited use of maternal appeals to unawareness of pregnancy's rhetorical force.) The ethical and emotional power of motherhood, then, played a relatively minor role in her opus to civil-rights workers, especially when compared to the rhetor's logical exposition.

Nash's objectives also help to explain why, upon entering the Hinds County Courthouse for her appeal hearing, she elected to sit in the white-only section of Judge Russell Moore's courtroom. Determined to contest segregation and enter jail one way or another, she refused to move to the colored section as ordered and immediately received a ten-day sentence for contempt of court.[2] After she finished serving the ten-day term, Judge Moore released Nash despite her assurances that she would return immediately to freedom fighting (Carson, *Student Voice* 53, 56). He eventually ruled that she could not abandon her appeal but then suspended her original sentence. Nash was, therefore, at liberty when she gave birth to her first child, Sherrilynn, on 5 August 1962 (Theoharis 835–36).[3]

Nash's appeal revocation (more specifically, the explanation presented in her letter and press release) may be viewed as a *rhetorical refusal*, "an act of writing or speaking in which the rhetor pointedly refuses to do what the audience considers rhetorically normal. By rejecting a procedure that the audience expects, the rhetor seeks the audience's assent to another principle, cast as a higher priority" (Schlib 3). Although it defies audience expectations, a rhetorical refusal, nevertheless, attempts to persuade even as it violates protocol. John Schlib characterizes such refusals as deliberate, purpose driven, and atypical (3), and Nash's decision to enter jail rather than cooperate further with Mississippi's "justice" system meets these criteria. It was a deliberate action, undertaken to set an example and change minds; it was purpose driven, intended to encourage arrested protesters to stay in jail; and it was atypical, defying established conventions of law, race, and gender. Regarding law, Nash's refusal moved counter to procedural assumptions that pursuing an appeal was preferable to going to jail. Regarding race, her negative assessment of Mississippi justice and voluntary incarceration flouted southern expectations of African Americans, who were "supposed" to accept the status quo uncritically, subserviently, and silently. Regarding gender, the expectant mother's willingness to enter prison violated norms of maternal conduct, which mandated that women prioritize pregnancy over politics and sequester themselves in the private sphere.

To elaborate on the latter refusal, Nash's press release addressed a national readership likely to uphold dominant gender conventions that positioned mothers within the home, encouraged their complete devotion to husband and children, and dictated their distance from public affairs; the soon-to-be mother's willingness to go to jail, dedication to civil rights, efforts to promote social justice, and immersion in public life clearly moved counter to those conventions. Furthermore, noncompliance with the code of motherhood had the potential to undermine Nash's ethos by positioning her toward the Woman, rather than the Mother, end of the rhetorical continuum (detailed in chapter 1). To recap briefly, the Mother operates as a god term within public discourse, connoting such positive associations as children, love, protection, altruism, morality, religion, self-sacrifice, strength, the reproductive body, and the nation; its corresponding devil term, Woman, brings to mind a variety of negative attributes, including self-centeredness, work, hysteria, irrationality, the sensual/sexual body, and the public sphere. A mother who fails to align herself with the god term risks ethical diminishment through association with the devil term.

Nash appeared to be sensitive to this possibility. To defend her decision to halt the appeals process, she argued that her unorthodoxy served a higher—and decidedly maternal—purpose, "hasten[ing] that day when my child and all children will be free, not only on the day of their birth but for all of their lives" ("Message" 1). Her enthymeme drew upon cultural assumptions about motherhood that were well known to audience members and, therefore, easily invoked through suggestion.[4] The "actual appeal" of an enthymeme, according to Susan Miller, derives from shared values that enable the rhetor to preclude mentioning "what everyone knows" and the audience to "provide the punchline" (67–68). Nash's enthymeme was rooted in beliefs about motherhood that, if fully stated, would run something like this:

Major Premise: Mothers do/should suffer for children's best interests.
Minor Premise: Nash is a (soon-to-be) Mother.
Conclusion: Therefore, Nash does/should suffer for children's best interests.

By drawing upon shared precepts about mothers, mothering, and motherhood, Nash framed her voluntary entry into prison as right conduct. She prioritized children's long-term well-being over their mothers' short-term comfort and successfully aligned herself with the god-term Mother (despite what, at first glance, appeared to be serious divergence from it). What is more, the enthymeme presented her self-sacrifice as noble (creating ethos), her courage as inspiring (creating pathos), and her decision as sensible (creating logos). The force of her maternal enthymeme, in fact, made it the most frequently cited excerpt from the press release and letter.

Nash, however, was not only a woman but also a person of color, which also informed the meaning and interpretation of her conduct. While her decision to enter jail while pregnant was likely perceived as a rhetorical refusal by audiences operating from within the dominant gender paradigm, it may well have seemed reasonable and responsible to those familiar with African-American traditions of mothering and motherhood. As Patricia Hill Collins explains, cultural assumptions that dichotomize "the public sphere of economic and political discourse and the private sphere of family and household responsibilities" have never reflected the lives of women of color, who routinely traversed those realms in the course of sustaining children and employment. Further, their maternal obligations encompassed both the personal and the communal, prompting them to safeguard their families while also ensuring "group survival, empowerment, and identity" (Collins, "Shifting" 58–59). To negotiate these duties, African-American women developed distinct maternal practices, serving as *bloodmothers* to their offspring, as *othermothers* to their kin's and neighbors' children, and as *community othermothers* to the larger black collective (Collins, *Black Feminist Thought* 189–92). The sense of social responsibility that accompanied these roles—particularly that of community othermother—prompted many educated black women to become politically active in the public sphere throughout the nineteenth and twentieth centuries (see Giddings, *When and Where*; Higginbotham; Logan).

Nash's appeal revocation, therefore, linked her to a long line of black women rhetors who coordinated motherwork with racial uplift and social justice. In the 1860s, for instance, both Frances Watkins Harper and

Mary Ann Shadd Cary combined mothering and public speaking, advocating abolition and emigration as well as recruiting black soldiers for the Union Army (see Buchanan, *Regendering* 177–78, 148–50). In 1896, antilynching crusader Ida B. Wells Barnett gave birth to her first child and almost immediately returned to the lecture circuit, remarking, "I honestly believe that I am the only woman in the United States who ever traveled throughout the country with a nursing baby to make political speeches" (qtd. in Giddings, *Ida* 377; Bay). As a result of black women's prominent, public roles as community othermothers, African-American standards of maternal decorum differed significantly from those of the dominant culture. To black audiences, then, Nash's entry into prison may well have appeared to be gender-as-usual rather than a gendered refusal.

As historians took note of Nash's appeal revocation and incorporated it into their accounts of the civil-rights movement, motherhood moved center stage and pushed the full scope and purpose of her resistant action into the shadows. Her portrayal as a courageous mother not only erased her strategic thinking and movement objectives but also disregarded her preferred rhetorical style. Ironically, although Nash enacted a rhetorical refusal that (for many) defied traditional maternal conventions, historians cast her as an exemplary Mother, and she has been remembered as such. Another source of distortion stemmed from their selective use of Nash's rhetoric: Writers who focused on maternal appeals and elided the legal, economic, and philosophical reasons underpinning jail-no-bail policy reduced her visionary act to a minor interlude in chronicles of Great Black Men of the Civil-Rights Movement. I turn to these accounts next.

Nash as Mother and Activist

Kimberlé Crenshaw provides a useful framework for examining representations of Nash's appeal revocation. She observes that women of color are positioned "within at least two subordinated groups that frequently pursue conflicting political agendas," namely, eradicating racism and obliterating sexism (1252). Antiracist (or civil-rights) groups typically make gendered assumptions that normalize black male experience while antisexist (feminist) groups make racial assumptions that normalize white women's experience. Both, therefore, "fail women of color by not acknowledging the 'additional' issue of race or of patriarchy" that constitutes their double burden. Furthermore, when either group disregards the concerns of the other, the "full dimensions of racism and sexism" are simplified, and the oppressive "power relations that each attempts to challenge are strengthened" (1282). Crenshaw encourages scholars to investigate depictions of African-American women and to identify how "prevalent narratives of race and gender" perpetuate their displacement (1282–83). Such representations matter because they either propagate or contest assumptions that have real consequences for women, history, and society.

I respond to Crenshaw's call for intersectional analysis by identifying underlying beliefs about race, gender, and motherhood embedded within historical accounts of Nash's appeal revocation and tracing their impact on her remembrance. Writers with an antiracist focus often presented her in ways that sustained patriarchy and cast the civil-rights movement as men's handiwork. They emphasized the activist's impending motherhood and ignored her efforts to encourage widespread adoption of jail-no-bail policy, thereby minimizing her strategic acumen and compromising her rightful recognition. Nash's marginalization transpired through a double movement: first, antiracist historians' perspective reinforced inequitable gender relations and, second, their allusions to the Mother flattened the accomplished and multifaceted organizer and projected a simple, authoritative stereotype in her place. Nash grew transparent through the tandem operations of antiracist history, which failed to acknowledge her position as a woman *and* person of color, and of the Mother, which partially consumed the woman even as it asserted a cultural ideal.

To appreciate the god term's impact in this case, one must recall that it reflects and sustains the entire network of power relations that undergird gender. Through constant repetition, the Mother presents the "social, the cultural, the ideological, [and] the historical" as natural, thereby converting the gender system's "contingent foundations" into "Common Sense, Right Reason, the Norm, General Opinion, in short the *doxa*" (Barthes, "Change the Object Itself" 165). Gendered *doxa* circulated untroubled and uncontested in antiracist accounts of Nash's appeal revocation. They depicted men and women in ways that naturalized motherhood, reified the gendered status quo, and sidelined the activist's organizational acumen and objectives. Roland Barthes's insights into connotation and denotation illuminate how historians' invocation of the god term encouraged Nash's commemoration as a mother, not a movement leader.

In his analysis of a *Paris Match* cover (see Figure 1.2), Barthes distinguishes between first- and second-order signification, the first order denoting a "black soldier . . . giving the French salute" and the second order extending and complicating the image's meaning through connotations of "Frenchness" and "militariness" (*Mythologies* 118). In similar fashion, antiracist portrayals of Nash denote a pregnant woman of color entering jail in order to protest racial injustice and simultaneously connote gendered *doxa* that, like the soldier's "Frenchness" and "militariness," tap into dominant maternal scripts, codes, and values. According to Barthes, the connotative form does not entirely suppress denotative meaning but "impoverishes it" and "puts it at a distance"; the denotative, thereby, "loses its value, but keeps its life," subsisting as the base from which connotation "draw[s] its nourishment" (118). The connotative form continually reroots itself in denotative meaning, and this "constant game of hide-and-seek" between the two is at the heart of their relationship. Therefore, even as the Negro soldier persists as "a rich, fully experienced, spontaneous, innocent, *indisputable* image," it is also "tamed, put at a distance, made almost transparent; it recedes a little, it becomes the accomplice of a concept which comes to it fully armed, French imperiality" (118). Nash—the young woman of color, the rhetor, the wife, the movement organizer—is likewise held hostage to the god-term Mother, which calls upon but then dismisses (and diminishes) the activist's richness and complexity. The Mother ultimately tames Nash, and the maternal attributes of courage, self-sacrifice, love, and morality displace logic, planning, and vision within the historical record.

With these considerations in mind, I turn to three representative accounts of Nash's appeal revocation, tracing their gendered assumptions and deployment of the Mother, their selective use of Nash's rhetoric, and their decontextualizing of her resistant action. I argue that they consistently subordinate Nash to the men around her through three narrative tropes—the essentialized exemplar, the giant fighter, and the good girl.

Manning Marable's *Race, Reform, and Rebellion: The Second Reconstruction and Beyond in Black America, 1945–2006* tracks advancement and retrenchment in race-related practices, policies, and politics over the course of six decades. Praising SNCC activists' grassroots efforts to "defy the segregation laws, to mobilize poor and working-class blacks in nonviolent demonstrations and to go to jail for their principles," Marable observes that it "is very difficult, in retrospect, to comprehend the sheer courage" of the "black teenagers and young adults" in the organization (64). To help readers grasp SNCC members' mettle, he introduces Nash and Bob Moses as exemplary "True Believers" of the civil-rights struggle. The writer employs a gendered framework to depict them both and begins by emphasizing his female protagonist's roles as a young wife and impending mother:

On 30 April 1962, Diane Nash Bevel, who had married activist James Bevel the year before, stood before a Mississippi court on charges of contributing to "juvenile delinquency"—she had taught black teenagers in McComb, Mississippi, the techniques needed for nonviolent demonstrations. Deliberately, she sat in the "whites-only" section of the courtroom. The angry judge sentenced the pregnant woman to serve ten days in the local jail for that single act of defiance. Nash responded, "I believe that if I go to jail it may help hasten that day when my child and all children will be free—not only on the day of their birth but for all of their lives." (64)

Marable paints Nash as a committed black activist, acknowledging her workshops on nonviolent resistance and her deliberate defiance of courtroom segregation. In response to the ten-day sentence imposed for that act, she expresses hope that her incarceration will improve conditions for her child and black children everywhere. No mention is made of her major objective, persuading the broader movement to embrace jail-without-bail policy. He also underscores gender by beginning with Nash's marriage to Bevel, mentioning her pregnancy three sentences in, and ending with the memorable enthymeme from her motherhood paragraph. Marable invokes the Mother by flagging Nash's courage and self-sacrifice for a higher principle—black children's well-being. Highlighting marriage, pregnancy, and motherhood within the space of four sentences foregrounds Nash's traditional performance of gender and casts her as a "feminine" True Believer.

Marable uses similar strategies to depict Moses, Nash's male counterpart, who tirelessly "organized voter registration drives in the face of tremendous white resistance" and, according to a bemused Mississippi resident, "took a lot of beatings": "He pioneered the way for black people. . . . He had more guts than any one man I've ever known" (64). Moses is cast as a devoted trailblazer, managing drives and registering voters despite savage white resistance. Like his biblical namesake, Moses leads the disenfranchised toward the Promised Land. He is clearly a "masculine" True Believer.

These gendered profiles in courage give readers a sense of SNCC members' moral fiber in the face of hostility and racism, a feat Marable accomplishes in the space of ten lines by presenting his exemplars in essentialized fashion—connecting Nash to marriage and motherhood and Moses to violence and fortitude. Because both characters inhabit conventional gender roles, they are immediately recognizable to cultural insiders, and their performance of femininity and masculinity renders those terms unproblematic. Marable might, instead, have demonstrated *Nash's* tenacity in the face of "tremendous white resistance." As coordinator of the sprawling Nashville sit-ins, she visited lunch counters across the city each day, checking on protesters and, on more than one occasion, encountering crowds of "hostile white people." Nash recalled a white spectator who "recognized me from my picture in the newspaper and said to his buddy, 'That's Diane Nash. She's the one to get'" (qtd. in Richardson 26). She was engulfed by a paralyzing "blanket of fear" as she realized that "somebody could stab me, and no one would really even see who did it" but conquered her terror sufficiently to continue coordinating the campaign. However, rather than acknowledging her fortitude in dangerous situations (a "masculine" attribute within his paradigm), Marable essentializes Nash and reinforces an inequitable gender system that privileges men over women. The historian's antiracist perspective explains his decisions to emphasize the activist's femininity and impending motherhood, to cite only her maternal enthymeme, and to jettison her arguments for jail-without-bail (thereby decontextualizing her efforts), rhetorical moves that diminish her dimensions and compromise her contributions to the civil-rights movement.

Other accounts employ a David-and-Goliath narrative and feature Nash in the role of *giant fighter*. They present a lone, pregnant woman of color who confronts a towering racist system and dares it to imprison her. Presuming that her incarceration would shine an unwelcome spotlight on southern bigotry, pregnancy is the sling and media attention the missile that topples the giant. This trope appears, for example, in Clayborne Carson's *In Struggle: SNCC and the Black Awakening of the 1960s*:

> At the hearing on April 30, she announced that, although expecting a child in the fall, she would drop her appeal of a conviction in the previous fall for contributing to the delinquency of minors. . . . She felt that she could no longer cooperate with Mississippi's "evil and unjust" court system, adding that her decision was the best thing she could do for her unborn child, since any black child born in Mississippi was already in prison: "I believe that if I go to jail now it may help hasten that day when my child and all children will be free—not only on the day of their birth but for all of their lives." Apparently unwilling to risk unfavorable publicity, the judge ruled that she could not abandon her appeal and suspended her sentence. Nonetheless she went to jail for ten days on a contempt charge for sitting in the white section of the courtroom. (68)

Carson's account presents a pregnant woman of color who resists racial injustice by choosing jail and a white judge who releases her (minus ten days for defying segregated courtroom seating) in order to avoid negative press. It suggests that Nash and the state are playing an elaborate race game and that her impending motherhood functions as a *Get Out of Jail Free* card. Pregnancy and publicity trump power and bigotry.[5]

Carson, like the other antiracist historians examined to this point, fails to mention the purpose of Nash's appeal revocation, encouraging the movement's return to jail-no-bail policy. He overlooks another important point as well. Bevel and Lafayette, Nash's SNCC colleagues in Mississippi, also incurred fines and jail time for "corrupting minors," and they, too, had their sentences suspended (Halberstam 394–95).[6] Accounts that ignore the similar treatment of Nash's male cohorts imply that pregnancy afforded her special privileges with the court. They also promote a variety of problematic gendered *doxa*, including, for example, that expectant women are volatile and vulnerable, that men are reasonable and women's natural protectors, that mothers do not belong in jail, in public, or in social protest. The upside of Carson's depiction (and gendered *doxa*) is that it aligns Nash's resistant action with the Mother's morality, nobility, self-sacrifice, and authority, creating admirable ethos; the downside is that it discourages her recognition as a strategist, for mothers presumably lack the qualities needed to influence organizational policy. Carson's antiracist focus produces an account that, on the one hand, features a young black woman leveling the giant of Mississippi racism but, on the other, promulgates gendered *doxa* that commemorate her motherhood, not her leadership, in the historical record.

The negative consequences of antiracist writers' insensitivity to gender are most apparent in Taylor Branch's *Pillar of Fire: America in the King Years, 1963–65*, which employs a third narrative trope, the good girl, and consistently subordinates Nash to the men around her. Branch begins by establishing her pregnancy, calling her "the young lady who [dared] Mississippi to make her give birth in jail." He then introduces a spiritual precept from Rev. James Lawson, whose workshop introduced Nash to nonviolent resistance and inspired her commitment to the Nashville sit-ins, namely, that "oppression requires the participation of the oppressed." The reverend's tenet, Branch explains, turned in his student's mind "until she saw her felony appeals as participation that soothed Mississippi with a false presumption of justice" (*Pillar* 55). The account suggests that Lawson's convictions prompted Nash's appeal revocation, a puzzling attribution as her press release and letter detail the spiritual principles and nonviolent imperatives guiding her action and give evidence of a formidable and independent thinker.

The historian then dramatizes a wildly confrontational courtroom scene that begins with Judge Moore banging "down an additional ten days for contempt when Nash refuse[s] to sit in the colored section of the courtroom." He describes the chaotic aftermath:

> Bevel, serving as her lawyer, made a speech to the court, and Nash herself read from an apocalyptic statement on why she chose to give birth behind bars. "This will be a black baby born in Mississippi," she declared before being led off to the Hinds County Jail, "and thus wherever he is born, he will be in prison. . . . I have searched my soul about this and considered it in prayer. I have reached the conclusion that in the long run, this will be the best thing I can do for my child." (*Pillar* 56)

Despite their revolutionary fervor, Bevel and Nash adopt fairly conventional gender roles: The husband handles legal matters, addressing the court on his wife's behalf, while she confines her remarks to pregnancy, childbirth, and progeny. Culling material from Nash's motherhood paragraph, Branch invokes the Mother and creates impressive ethos for the activist, portraying her as a brave, self-sacrificing woman of color who voluntarily delivers herself into racist hands in order to benefit her child and the larger black collective. He makes no mention of her efforts to persuade arrested protestors to stay in jail and forego bail, an omission that presents Nash chiefly as Bevel's expectant wife; undercuts her agency, agenda, and acumen; and relegates her to a supporting role. Branch's vivid, memorable, moving courtroom scene is also inaccurate: Nash was represented by a lawyer, not her husband, during the hearing and was not permitted to utter a word, making delivery of an "apocalyptic statement" about birth behind bars impossible (Nash, 2008 interview).

The troubling gender assumptions embedded within Branch's narrative emerge even more strongly in the next scene. After Nash is dragged off to jail, the setting shifts to the judge's chambers, where Moore and Bevel debate principles and priorities. The judge urges the husband to protect his young, vulnerable, pregnant wife and insists that Bevel's "first duty in all his roles—as lay attorney, citizen, husband, and expectant father—is to keep Nash out of prison, not in it":

"You know, son," he said ruefully, "you people are insane."

"Judge Moore, you don't understand Christianity," Bevel replied. "All the early Christians went to jail."

"Maybe so," said the judge. "But they weren't all pregnant and twenty-one." Bevel held his ground during the standoff, assuring Moore that Nash would renounce any court-appointed lawyer who tried to reinstate her appeal. Moore eventually ordered her release and simply ignored the uncontested two-year sentence. (Branch, *Pillar* 56)

By this point in the story, Nash has become the silent, offstage object of men's negotiation, her maternal body configured as a site of racial contention. Bevel wins the battle, holding "his ground during the standoff" through willingness to keep his wife in jail, and Nash's release and suspended sentence stem from the judge's somewhat confused sense of chivalry. Throughout Branch's account, Nash is presented as a good girl—a faithful student, a trusting wife, an idealistic mother-to-be—whose actions are determined by the men in her life. Branch's antiracist agenda not only reifies gender hierarchy but also attributes civil-rights advances to men like Bevel, Martin Luther King, Ralph Abernathy, Fred Shuttlesworth, and Medgar Evers. In the process, the good girl is reduced to their courageous, committed sidekick.

Marable, Carson, and Branch's primary interest in racial politics, repetition of gendered *doxa*, and rendition of motherhood erase Nash's efforts to steer movement policy on this occasion. Granted, their invocations of the Mother create impressive ethos for Nash and dramatic accounts of the event. However, their appeals derive chiefly from the rhetor's motherhood paragraph (which is cited by all three) while everything else in the press release and letter, including her rationale for halting the appeals process, goes unmentioned. Without philosophical ground, organizational purpose, or movement context, Nash's resistant action is moving and unforgettable but, ultimately, somewhat pointless. Such elisions, Crenshaw observes, occur whenever race or gender becomes the sole concern, in either case relegating "women of color to a location that resists telling" (1242). Branch's account reveals this process at work most clearly, its antiracist focus presenting Nash as a good girl, student, wife, and mother rather than an independent agent, thinker, strategist, or leader. She is finally relegated to a "location that resists telling," rendered voiceless and invisible as men debate and decide her future. They, not she, would be remembered in the history books.

Nash as Wife and Collaborator

I have argued that antiracist depictions of Nash's appeal revocation emphasized conventional femininity and motherhood and played a role in delaying recognition of her contributions as a civil-rights strategist and organizer. There was, however, yet another way in which maternity contributed to her historical displacement. Motherhood, after all, operates not only as a topos that generates means of persuasion or a god term that encodes dominant gender ideals but also as a cultural code that shapes women's daily lives and practices. Nash, Lynne Olson observes, was unquestionably "one of the most daring, creative, committed" leaders of the early movement, but she was also a young woman who grew up "in the conservative 1950s" (212). Raised with "the notion that a wife should defer to her husband, even if that wife once had stood up to the President and Attorney General of the United States," she believed that a mother's place was at home with her children (Olsen 212). The activist, therefore, left the front lines of the movement following the August 1962 birth of daughter Sherilynn, who was soon followed by son Douglass. The code of motherhood, then, also influenced Nash's rhetorical production and participation in civil-rights campaigns.

I documented motherhood's disruptive impact on women's civic engagement and public discourse in *Regendering Delivery: The Fifth Canon and Antebellum Women Rhetors*, examining its capacity to halt their vocations as lecturers, interrupt their work "for periods ranging from months to years" (127), or delay the start of their careers until after their children were grown. These patterns were evident, for example, in the lives of Frances Wright, Angelina Grimké Weld, Abby Kelley Foster, Antoinette Brown Blackwell, Frances Watkins Harper, Isabella Beecher Hooker, Elizabeth Cady Stanton, and Ida Wells Barnett. Motherhood limited nineteenth-century women's discursive production and delivery, and it continues to constrain maternal rhetors to this day.

Nash, like many of her foremothers, relinquished direct public involvement following the birth of her children although retirement did not end her contributions to the civil-rights movement. From home, she continued to strategize major initiatives with her husband, including the 1963 Birmingham desegregation campaign, the 1963 March on Washington for Jobs and Freedom, and the 1965 Alabama voting-rights campaign ("Nash," n.p.). The couple alternated pitching their ideas to movement leaders, but Bevel typically coordinated their projects in the field while Nash remained home with the children (see Figure 3.2). This collaboration linked her, once again, to earlier generations of women, whose partnerships with friends, family, and servants enabled them to negotiate conflicting maternal and civic obligations, produce and deliver rhetoric, and gain access to public forums (see Buchanan, *Regendering* 131–40).

The genesis of the 1965 Alabama voting-rights campaign illustrates the nature and effectiveness of the Nash/Bevel collaboration. The impetus for the project, she later explained, was the 1963 dynamiting of Birmingham's Sixteenth Street Baptist Church, which resulted in the deaths of four young girls:

> My former husband and I . . . cried when we heard about the bombing, because in many ways we felt like our own children had been killed. . . . We decided that we would do something about it, and we said that we had two options. First, we felt confident that if we tried, we could find out who had done it, and we could make sure they got killed. We considered that as a real option. The second option was that we felt that if blacks in Alabama had the right to vote, they could protect black children. We deliberately made a choice, and chose the second option. (qtd. in Hampton and Fayer 173)

Figure 3.2. Nash and her husband, James Bevel (1963). Wisconsin Historical Society, WHi-91969.

The couple proceeded to "draw up an initial strategy draft" for a voter-registration campaign in Alabama. Nash then boarded a plane, attended the four girls' funeral, and met with movement leaders to urge adoption of the Alabama plan. It developed into the Selma and Lowndes County voting-rights campaign, one of the most compelling and successful civil-rights drives, and spurred passage of the Voting Rights Act of 1965, which guaranteed all citizens the right to vote, regardless of race (Branch, *Pillar* 139–41; also see Branch, *At Canaan's Edge*).

Nash's collaboration with her husband enabled her to participate in and contribute to the movement after her children's arrival. There were, however, serious disadvantages to the arrangement. For one, her efforts were generally overlooked while his reputation soared within the civil-rights community. As SNCC organizer Ivanhoe Donaldson observed, Bevel eclipsed Nash following their marriage, and she "faded into his background while his star was out there shining" (qtd. in Olson 211). SCLC's Andrew Young belatedly acknowledged Nash's part in the couple's projects, noting that "no small measure of what we saw as Jim's brilliance was due to Diane's rational thinking and influence" (342). Because SCLC ministers "were not advocates for women's equality at this stage," they equated Nash's behind-the-scenes contributions with those of their wives, who ran "the choir," "Sunday school," and "women's fellowship without any compensation" but their husbands' salaries: "It is not to our credit that we followed that model with Diane" (Young 342). SNCC's and SCLC's disregard of Nash's collaborative role contributed to her sidelining in movement history.

The collaboration had other negative, long-term ramifications for Nash. In 1968, she divorced Bevel and relocated to Chicago with her children. Having abandoned her studies in 1960 in order to devote herself to desegregation, Nash lacked a college degree. She soon realized that her sacrifices for and collaborative contributions to civil rights carried little cachet in the world:

> Bevel, as the man, and as the more visible member of the team, had gotten most of the credit for what they had done. That had not bothered her at the time, for the mission itself had always been more important than the glory . . . , but now that she was out trying to support her family, it had become a factor. By her estimates Bevel's earning power was about three and a half times hers. (Halberstam 631)

Despite Bevel's relative prosperity, Nash raised and supported Sherilynn and Douglass on her own, and they all suffered economically for her youthful idealism, naiveté, and humility. Finances would prove "hard, extremely demanding, indeed exacting" for the remainder of Nash's life (Halberstam 631).

The code of motherhood, then, shaped Nash's rhetorical practice in significant ways. Her retirement from direct movement involvement following the birth of her children and subsequent collaboration with Bevel connected her to a long line of American women rhetors, who likewise struggled to reconcile maternity with public life. Withdrawal from the limelight to raise children, behind-the-scenes work with her husband, and institutional sexism within civil-rights organizations: each of these elements also contributed to Nash's elision from cultural memory—at least for a time.

Recuperating the Movement Leader

Women's contributions to civil rights are, at long last, receiving recognition thanks to intersectional scholarship that considers the interplay of race, gender, class, region, and religion on movement participants, initiatives, and events. These works include Bettye Collier-Thomas and V. P. Franklin's *Sisters in the Struggle: African-American Women in the Civil Rights–Black Power Movement*; Vicki Crawford, Jacqueline Anne Rouse, and Barbara Woods's *Women in the Civil Rights Movement: Trailblazers and Torchbearers, 1941–1965*; Davis W. Houck and David E. Dixon's *Women and the Civil Rights Movement, 1954–1965*; Peter J. Ling and Sharon Monteith's *Gender and the Civil Rights Movement*; Lynne Olson's *Freedom's Daughters: The Unsung Heroines of the Civil Rights Movement from 1830 to 1970*; Belinda Robnett's *How Long? How Long? African-American Women in the Struggle for Civil Rights*; and Rosetta Ross's *Witnessing and Testifying: Black Women, Religion, and Civil Rights*. In consequence, more nuanced examinations of Nash's appeal revocation are now appearing that acknowledge her pregnancy *and* underlying motives. Reclaiming the rhetor's reasons and objectives, long hidden beneath the mantle of motherhood, is an important step in redressing gender imbalances and distortions within the historical record.

Belinda Robnett has produced the most comprehensive account of the incident to date, and it is particularly instructive, first, for its recuperation of Nash's strategic purpose and acumen and, second, for its positioning of the activist within the mainstream movement. Like Marable, Carson, and Branch, Robnett addresses and even foregrounds Nash's pregnancy but resists the temptation to present her solely in that light. Instead, the writer incorporates complexities ignored elsewhere and attends to context in ways that direct the spotlight away from the Mother and onto Diane Nash, the woman of color, the SNCC organizer and tactician, the wife and impending mother. Robnett accomplishes this by connecting Nash's decision to enter jail with promotion of jail-no-bail policy and by situating that action within the wider movement. In fact, she identifies Martin Luther King as Nash's primary rhetorical audience.

Robnett begins by acknowledging women's frequently overlapping roles as activists and mothers: "Just like their male comrades, women risked their lives for the movement. Some even risked the lives of their children" (106). She then introduces Nash, establishing her marriage to Bevel and pregnancy of four months. The writer details the nature of Nash's pending charges for "contributing to the delinquency of minors" but greatly condenses events, simply relating that she "was sentenced to two years' imprisonment but served only ten days" (106–7).[7] Robnett segues from Nash's incarceration to King's participation in and arrest for a 16 December 1961 desegregation march in Albany, Georgia. Although the minister announced his determination to stay in jail, he bailed out soon after, a decision that deeply disappointed SNCC organizers spearheading the Albany campaign. Robnett frames Nash's advocacy of jail-without-bail policy as a response to King's departure from his Albany cell and cites an extended passage from the rhetor's 30 April 1962 letter to civil-rights workers. With this background in place, readers can almost hear Nash speaking directly to King:

> I believe the time has come, and is indeed long past, when each of us must make up his mind, when arrested on unjust charges, to serve his sentence and stop posting bonds. I believe that unless we do this our movement loses its power and will never succeed. We in the nonviolent movement have been talking about jail without bail for two years or more. It is time for us to mean what we say. (qtd. in Robnett 107)

Robnett includes eleven sentences from Nash's letter, integrating material *other* than the oft-cited motherhood paragraph. In the process, Nash's philosophical and organizational arguments for jail-no-bail policy (a term absent in Marable's, Carson's, and Branch's versions) and penchant for logical exposition become audible. Nine of eleven sentences present reasons for arrested protesters to forego bond while only two concern Nash's pregnancy. Compared to antiracist accounts of the event, Robnett devotes far less space and attention to the rhetor's impending motherhood (although its placement at the episode's beginning and end make the point memorable). The writer also links Nash's pregnancy to her policy objectives and situates her letter within the broad trajectory of the civil-rights movement. Arguing for the effectiveness of the rhetor's discourse and action, Robnett attributes King's subsequent decision to return to and serve his sentence in the Albany jail to Nash's influence.[8] This rich, contextualized, intersectional analysis produces a well-rounded portrait of Nash as an activist contesting racial injustice and a woman within a male-dominated organization. Robnett's attention to the dynamics of race and gender makes motherhood *an* element, rather than *the* element, of the narrative. Nash emerges from out of the shadows and can be recognized for her impact on the movement.

My examination of Nash's appeal revocation reveals how motherhood impacted her public discourse, historical remembrance, and rhetorical career and facilitated her marginalization in official accounts of the civil-rights movement. Motherhood's paradoxical capacity to generate rhetorical resources but reduce women to gendered stereotypes comes fully into focus here. Nash's maternal appeals made her action moving, memorable, and understandable to others; however, they also displaced her advocacy of jail-without-bail policy in many histories, which commemorated a courageous African-American mother but elided the proponent of nonviolent resistance, the spiritual practitioner, and the movement strategist. Antiracist historians flattened the multifaceted woman of color by invoking the god-term Mother and its constellation of positive attributes that are immediately recognizable and deeply meaningful to cultural insiders. Furthermore, the code of motherhood influenced Nash's rhetorical practice, prompting her retirement from public life following the birth of her children and her behind-the-scenes collaboration with Bevel on major initiatives. Motherhood, thus, shaped history and praxis in ways that undermined recognition of Nash's leadership role in and strategic contributions to the civil-rights movement.

Despite intersectional scholars' recuperative efforts, there is still a long way to go before Nash receives her due, as was apparent on the fifty-year anniversary of the Freedom Rides. In May 2011, a five-day reunion and conference took place in Jackson, Mississippi, featuring an extensive series of lectures, exhibits, tours, celebrations, and show-ings. The name *Diane Nash*, however, did not appear once among the scheduled events, list of Riders, or historical blurbs featured on the event website (see *Return of the Freedom Riders, 50th Anniversary Reunion*). Disregarding the organizer who not only revived the Freedom Rides after violence brought them to a halt but also coordinated their final leg into Jackson reflects the snail-like pace of women's integration into cultural memory.

Cheryl Glenn assures feminist historiographers that "history is not frozen" and, instead, presents "an approachable, disruptable ground for engaging and transforming traditional memory . . . in the interest of both the present and future" ("Comment" 463). With this hope, I have detailed the process of Nash's marginalization, confident that unveil-ing gendered, raced, and maternal obstructions can unsettle history, as Glenn suggests, and make it fairer to and more inclusive of women.

4

Changing Constructs of Motherhood:
Pregnancy and Personhood in Laci and Conner's Law

> Any time an expectant mother is a victim of violence, two lives
> are in the balance, each deserving protection, and each deserv-
> ing justice. If the crime is murder and the unborn child's life
> ends, justice demands a full accounting under the law. . . . All
> who knew Laci Peterson have mourned two deaths, and the law
> cannot look away and pretend there was just one.
>
> —George W. Bush

With these words and a flourish of the pen, President George W. Bush signed Laci and Conner's Law: The Unborn Victims of Violence Act (UVVA), the congressional bill named to honor Laci Peterson, an eight-months-pregnant woman heinously killed by her husband, Scott, in 2002. Bush identified both the "expectant mother" and "unborn child" as victims and argued that Peterson's murder resulted in "two deaths," rather than one, each meriting "protection," "justice," and "a full accounting under the law" ("Remarks" n.p.). In signing the UVVA and making it law, he significantly revised the U.S. Criminal Code to recognize pregnant women *and* the unborn as separate victims of violent crime, thereby introducing fetal rights into federal statutes for the first time and tracing the inception of personhood to conception, not birth or viability. Passage of the UVVA, therefore, marked a major victory for the antiabortion movement, which had worked patiently for decades to modify state and federal law in precisely this manner. Samuel Casey, former executive director of the Christian Legal Society, explains why: "In as many areas as we can, we want to put on the books that the embryo is a person. That sets the stage for a jurist to acknowledge that human beings at any stage of development deserve protection, even protection that would trump a woman's interest in terminating a pregnancy" (qtd.

in House H661). One of the ways that antiabortionists extended legal protections to the unborn (and rendered their civic standing comparable to that of the women carrying them) was through crime bills like the UVVA; it added a critical federal component to a growing body of state statutes designed to challenge *Roe v Wade*, the 1973 Supreme Court ruling that legalized abortion in the United States. Laci and Conner's Law, then, was ultimately less concerned with curtailing violence against pregnant women than with granting citizenship rights to the contents of their wombs.

The UVVA also exemplified a new phase in the social and rhetorical meaning of motherhood. As I detailed in chapter 1, the construct is culturally specific, historically variable, and contextually bound. Traditionally, pregnancy has been framed as a holistic process that unfolds within a woman's body over the course of nine months and culminates in the birth of a living person and legal subject. The conviction that personhood begins *after* birth has, in fact, been legally encoded for more than a millennium in the form of the "born-alive rule." This legal precedent, however, has come under increasing fire since the early 1960s when new medical and imaging technologies, including ultrasound and intrauterine photography, began to reconfigure pregnancy in the public imaginary.[1] As Celeste Condit explains in *Decoding Abortion Rhetoric*, fetal imagery provided the antiabortion movement with graphic and compelling resources for arguing that personhood began *prior* to birth. Through a variety of visual strategies, antiabortionists transformed public perceptions of the unborn, reshaping them from dependent, developing life forms carried by expectant women into independent, vulnerable children in the womb (whose female hosts were elided more often than not) (Condit 82–85).[2] Consequently, the "organic unity" of pregnancy has been displaced by the uneasy cohabitation of two separate subjects, a preborn child and female sponsor, within a single body (Daniels 1, 3). Feminists scholars—including Cynthia Daniels, Fay Duden, Lynn Morgan and Meredith Michaels, Rachel Roth, Rebecca Stringer, and Rosalind Petchesky among others—have announced the birth of a new rhetorical figure, the *public fetus*, which now functions as the "tiniest citizen" and central "'social actor' in the American conservative imagination" (Daniels 3). Conservatives' appropriation of the public fetus has resulted in legal rulings and policy decisions that endow the unborn with rights potentially in conflict with those of the women who carry them.

The changing depictions and perceptions of pregnancy identified above constitute a new development in motherhood's signification.

After all, motherhood and pregnancy are not imbued with stable, inherent meaning; they are, instead, shot through with cultural, ideological, and emotional connotations that are constantly being (re)defined within the social body. Further, as Rebecca Kukla so rightly cautions, the ways in which these constructs are conceptualized, represented, and deployed have serious "ethical, political, practical, and medical repercussions" for women (4). Sensitive to Kukla's admonition, this chapter examines how pregnant women and the unborn were imagined and personhood presented in congressional debate about the UVVA, a rich locus for charting motherhood's current manifestation in public discourse. Proponents of the bill (chiefly Republicans opposed to abortion) depicted pregnancy as a two-person condition, thereby attributing legal personhood and civic rights to the unborn. UVVA rhetors also enjoyed full access to the motherhood topos, and their moving accounts of *mothers* and *unborn children*, ironically enough, helped ensure passage of legislation that jeopardizes women's control over when and whether to give birth. Meanwhile, those who opposed the bill (chiefly pro-choice Democrats) employed a conventional one-person paradigm of pregnancy and carefully refrained from engaging with or imputing personhood to the fetus. Their inability either to refute UVVA rhetoric or to produce equally compelling discourse of their own stemmed, in large measure, from the pro-choice movement's refusal to accept changing constructs of pregnancy, particularly the public fetus. Its stance has had adverse results, and, as coming analysis of congressional debate shows, does not bode well for the future of women's reproductive rights in the United States. These stakes indicate the significant legal, political, medical, and material consequences that follow from motherhood's representation and use in public discourse.[3]

How does this chapter advance my study of rhetorics of motherhood? The previous two chapters on Margaret Sanger and Diane Nash may be viewed as flipsides of a coin, illustrating both the positive and negative outcomes of women rhetors' alignment with the god-term Mother. In Sanger's case, the move helped her to push controversial matters, including radicalism and law breaking, into the background and to present a comforting maternal face to the public. Foregrounding motherhood enabled her to repair damaged ethos and attract women to the burgeoning cause of birth control. In Nash's case, the same move permitted her to create a moving, memorable justification of her appeal revocation; however, historians' fixation on her maternal appeals minimized the activist's strategic acumen and organizational accomplishments and led to her marginalization in accounts of the civil-rights movement. Like the Sanger and Nash case studies, this one also addresses the construct of motherhood but focuses, in particular, on its changing figuration in the political forum and potential consequences for women. I begin by exploring the issue of legal personhood and its recent extension to the unborn in state and federal statutes; I, then, turn to rhetorical representations of pregnancy and personhood in House and Senate deliberations concerning the UVVA.

Definitional Stasis: Personhood

The central dispute of the abortion controversy concerns legal personhood—when it begins, what it entails, how it is defined. Definitions, as Edward Schiappa explains in *Defining Reality: Definitions and the Politics of Meaning*, are "introduced or contested" whenever one wants "to alter others' linguistic behavior in a particular fashion," reshape their "understanding of the world," or revise their "attitudes and behaviors" (32). Definitions are, therefore, socially constructed, value laden, epistemic, and "rhetorically induced," a term that highlights "the persuasive processes that definitions inevitably involve" (3). It is not surprising to learn that rhetors have debated the meaning of personhood for millennia, attempting to convince others of the values, assumptions, and perspectives embedded within their own definitions of the term.[4]

The legal definition of personhood initially emerged from the English common-law tradition, which held that the fetus did not exist as a rights-bearing person until, and unless, it was born alive. Live birth, then, has conventionally marked the beginning of legal personhood. This precedent, often described as the "born-alive rule," was followed in the United States but came under scrutiny in *Dietrich v. Northampton* (1884), a suit filed on behalf of a pregnant woman who miscarried "as a result of a defect in the town highway" and subsequently sued the town of Northampton for damages (Daniels 10). Justice Oliver Wendell Holmes, writing for the Massachusetts Supreme Court, identified the case's central question as "whether an infant dying before it was able to live separated from its mother could be said to have become a person recognized by the law as capable of having a *locus standi* in court." Legal action, he explained, was dependent upon the child having achieved "some degree of quasi independent life," so the justice denied an award to the woman, reasoning that the fetus was "a part of the mother at the time of the injury" (10–11). Holmes concluded that "the unborn fetus had been lost 'before he became a person,'" thereby revisiting but upholding the born-alive rule.

In matters of inheritance, however, courts were willing to acknowledge the property rights of the unborn provided it was subsequently born alive: "A fetus could inherit property upon its birth even though the fetus did not technically exist as a person at the time of death of its benefactor" (Daniels 11). The divergent judgments rendered in prenatal injury and inheritance cases stemmed from differing definitions of personhood, the "basic dichotomy" revolving around whether the unborn was considered to be "a 'part' of the mother or a 'separate, distinct, and individual' entity" (Wellman 78–79). Nineteenth-century law typically framed the fetus as "part" of the pregnant woman in damage cases and, provisionally, as a "distinct" entity in inheritance cases (again, provided it was eventually born alive).

The issue of fetal personhood landed on the Supreme Court's doorstep in 1971 in the form of *Roe v. Wade*, a suit challenging the state of Texas's restrictive abortion regulations. The Court had to determine whether or not the fetus was entitled to constitutional protections under the Fourteenth Amendment, which holds that states may not "deprive any person of life, liberty, or property, without due process of law" or deny "any person within its jurisdiction the equal protection of the laws" ("Fourteenth," n.p.). If the fetus was recognized as a legal subject, its right to life would be guaranteed by the Fourteenth Amendment. *Roe* attorney Sarah Weddington argued that both legal precedent and the Court's own decisions suggested that the unborn did not qualify as legal persons because such rights began only at birth. The Court reviewed medical research on pregnancy and concluded that it did not "establish that a fetus was a human being from the instant of conception" but instead indicated that "coming to be a human being was a process" (Condit 110). The born-alive rule, therefore, survived intact (although the Court described the unborn as "a substance of value" that deserved state protection after reaching the point of viability). The 7–2 *Roe v Wade* decision acknowledged the central importance of fetal personhood and noted that if it were ever firmly established, the opinion would collapse (410 U.S. 113 [1973], IX: A, 20–22).[5]

Although state legislatures and Congress must respect the High Court's ruling, they can challenge its legal basis—the born-alive rule. Since the *Roe* decision, antiabortion groups have lobbied to redefine personhood in both state and federal law, inching its traditional inception at birth back to an earlier point in the gestational process. State and federal statutes that recognize fetal personhood suggest that the unborn possess constitutionally protected rights, create alternate precedent to the born-alive rule, and establish legal grounds for testing the landmark *Roe* decision. Passing or defeating such measures has, therefore, become one of the foremost fields of contention in the continuing battle over abortion.

Laci and Conner's Law was a single, albeit extremely important, episode in an antiabortion campaign of long duration, one that sought to modify the personhood status of the unborn in criminal law. Historically, criminal code followed common-law tradition and granted only born persons status as murder victims, thus affording no protection for pregnancies that ended due to violence. Serious shortcomings unquestionably resulted from laws that made harming a pregnant woman justiciable but ignored injury to or death of a viable, late-term fetus.[6] To address such oversights, legislators had two options. First, they could modify crime statutes and impose enhanced sentencing penalties for assault against a pregnant woman that resulted in miscarriage, a measure that provided compensation for the woman's extra loss (Roth 11). Such measures continued to acknowledge only the woman as a victim of violent crime but increased consequences for injury to or termination of a pregnancy, closing loopholes but leaving the born-alive ruling intact. Legislators' second option was to enact laws that recognized and imposed sentencing penalties for harm done to two victims, in effect overturning common-law tradition and creating a new category of crime, feticide. Critics protested that two-victim crime statutes not only failed to compensate a pregnant woman for her loss but also redefined the fetus as an independent legal entity (Roth 11–12). Granting the unborn status as "a law-worthy 'victim,'" of course, also suggested it was "a rights-bearing subject" (Stringer 9), a proposition with troubling long-term implications for women's reproductive choice. Despite this possibility, most states pursued the second option and passed two-victim crime legislation, in many cases, as a result of intense lobbying efforts by antiabortion groups.

California was the first state to grant the fetus victim status, in 1970 amending its penal code to read, "Murder is the unlawful killing of a human being, or a fetus, with malice aforethought" ("State Homicide Laws," n.p.). Michigan acknowledged the killing of an "unborn quick child" as manslaughter in 1973, and Minnesota expanded murder or manslaughter charges to include "the unborn child at any stage of development" in 1989. Only three states passed fetal homicide laws between 1970 and 1990, but a flurry of activity has followed since. By the end of the 1990s, seventeen states recognized "the unlawful killing of an unborn child as homicide in at least some circumstances," and that number reached thirty-six in May 2011 ("State Homicide Laws," n.p.).

Changing state legislation created new precedent in court cases involving the fetus, as was apparent, for example, in *Aka v. Jefferson Hospital Association* (2001). In 1995, the Arkansas Supreme Court ruled that parents could not initiate wrongful death suits on behalf of the unborn; however, it reversed itself six years later in *Aka* on the basis of recent modifications to the state constitution (which committed Arkansas to protecting "the life of every unborn child from conception until birth, to the extent permitted by the Federal Constitution") and to state crime laws (which recognized the "killing of an 'unborn child' of twelve weeks or greater gestation" as murder, manslaughter, or negligent homicide) (Marzilli 48; "State Homicide Laws," n.p.). According to the court, the legislature had "nullified the common law restriction" and freed the Akas to "sue the doctors and hospital for wrongful death after the stillbirth of their child" (Marzilli 48). Once a substantial body of legislative actions and court decisions acknowledge fetal personhood in similar fashion, it can be used to challenge *Roe v. Wade*.

Laci and Conner's Law: The Unborn Victims of Violence Act added a federal component to a growing assortment of state feticide statutes. When Melissa Hart (R-PA) and Mike DeWine (R-OH) respectively introduced the bill to the House and Senate, they noted a "deficiency," "omission," or "gap" in federal crime laws that granted only born subjects status as murder victims and thus afforded no protection to fetuses that died due to violence. Their bill sought to remedy that "deficiency" by acknowledging two victims—the pregnant woman and the unborn—in cases of violent crime. Its scope was limited, applying only to murders or acts of violence that occurred on military bases, while federal crimes were underway, or in federal jurisdictions, such as national parks, military facilities, or Washington, D.C. (Marzilli 18, 53); in all other circumstances and settings, state homicide laws applied. The UVVA was controversial for two reasons: first, because it sought to revise the U.S. Criminal Code to recognize both the pregnant woman and the fetus as independent victims and, second, because of its definition of the unborn victim. According to the bill, anyone who, in the process of harming a pregnant woman, inflicted bodily injury on or caused the death of "a child in utero" would be guilty of a second criminal offense. The UVVA defined the "child in utero" or "unborn child" as "a member of the species homo sapiens, at any stage of development, . . . in the womb," granting rights to the unborn from the moment of conception (House H638).

Although the bill acknowledged both the pregnant woman and the unborn as separate, rights-bearing subjects, proponents argued that it posed no threat to reproductive choice due to three exemptions: abortions to which pregnant women consented, medical treatment for a pregnant woman and/or fetus, and consequences of a pregnant woman's actions with regard to the fetus. Nevertheless, alarm over the UVVA's potential ramifications prompted introduction of an alternate bill, the Motherhood Protection Act (MPA), by Zoe Lofgren (D-CA) in the House and Dianne Feinstein (D-CA) in the Senate. Designed to avert the dangers that two-victim federal legislation presented to *Roe*, the MPA recognized only the pregnant woman as a crime victim but imposed enhanced sentencing penalties for violence that caused "termination of pregnancy or interruption of the normal course of pregnancy" due to prenatal injuries (Senate S3125). The one-victim bill, then, provided consequences for two separate crimes but kept the born-alive rule intact. With this background on personhood, abortion, and feticide law in place, I turn to congressional deliberation about the one- and two-victim crime bills.

Pregnancy, Personhood, and Persuasion

As the bills' titles suggest, motherhood was a central trope in House and Senate debate over Laci and Conner's Law and the Motherhood Protection Act. That trope, however, was not equally available to speakers on both sides of the aisle. MPA supporters (who were pro-choice Democrats) were seriously constrained due to their one-person construct of pregnancy, their conviction that women's rights took precedence over fetal rights, and their contention that personhood began at birth. To promote one-victim legislation, they emphasized *women* (rather than *mothers* or *unborn children*) and foregrounded the threat the UVVA posed to reproductive choice. These choices made good sense but had profoundly negative rhetorical consequences, confining pro-choice rhetors chiefly to logos, minimizing opportunities for pathos, and damaging ethos. Calling their bill the Motherhood Protection Act was, in fact, one of their few successful uses of the trope, enabling them to shift the focus from unborn victims of violence to pregnant women and to tap into maternity's rich valences.

UVVA proponents (who were predominantly Republicans opposed to abortion) employed a two-person paradigm of pregnancy that gave them full recourse to the motherhood topos and god-term Mother. As I explained in discussion of the Woman/Mother continuum in chapter 1, the god term connotes positive cultural associations, including children, home, love, empathy, protection, nourishment, altruism, morality, religion, self-sacrifice, strength, reproduction, and the nation. The Mother's antithesis is the Woman, a devil term linked to such negative attributes as self-centeredness, childlessness, work, hysteria, irrationality, the sensual/sexual body, and the public sphere. The Woman/Mother continuum gives rhetors persuasive avenues for praising or castigating, promoting or undermining people and policies by affiliating them with either the god or devil term. UVVA proponents aligned their efforts to recognize the fetus as an independent crime victim with the Mother, framing themselves and their bill as protectors of the young and showing both in a flattering light. They also suggested, directly and indirectly, that opponents of the UVVA were unconcerned with motherhood, thereby associating MPA advocates with the Woman end of the continuum and eroding their ethos.

Above all, UVVA rhetors moved audiences through their figuration of pregnancy as a two-person condition, involving both a *mother* and *preborn child*. Emotions, Aristotle observed, "are those things through which, by undergoing change, people come to differ in their judgments" (2.1.8). The discipline of rhetoric, however, has often been suspicious of pathos, framing it "as the unfortunate third persuasive appeal in Aristotle's *Rhetoric*" (Miller 13); equating it with "manipulation, excess, and irrationality" (Micciche xiii); and collapsing it with "all things feminine" (and, therefore, characterizing it as "weak, shallow, petty, vain, and narcissistic") (Micciche 3, 6–7). Rhetorical scholars have begun to reconceptualize the meaning and function of feeling in such works as Lynn Worsham's "Going Postal: Pedagogic Violence and the Schooling of Emotions," Laura Micciche's *Doing Emotion: Rhetoric, Writing, and Teaching*, and Susan Miller's *Trust in Texts: A Different History of Rhetoric*. Micciche envisions emotion as a "valuable rhetorical resource" that "generates attachments to others, to world-views, and to a whole array of sources and objects" (1). Miller, meanwhile, identifies feelings as social, not personal, artifacts, whose causes and significance are contextually determined: Emotion "arises from cultural scripts that are never entirely outside the ken" of those who have been taught to recognize, honor, and trust them (21). After all, subjects are educated into a common matrix of scripts, codes, and roles and subsequently unite around shared "standards of credible behavior," "fitting responses to specific situations," and "appropriate ways of talking about them" (22). That schooling, Miller argues, promotes a sense of community grounded in emotion and its corollary, trust (23). A rhetor and her audience, therefore, must hold in common (or discover) codes that stir shared emotions and stimulate trust *before* persuasion becomes possible.

Miller's perspective not only unsettles a foundational rhetorical precept holding that emotion follows from, rather than precedes, persuasion but also illuminates motherhood's capacity to invoke strong feeling. Motherhood is part of the dominant system of gender, and enculturation requires subjects to learn "standards of credible behavior" by and toward mothers, the role's associations and expectations, as well as "appropriate ways" of discussing maternity. To those indoctrinated to its cultural place and meaning, the code of motherhood invites, perhaps even demands, particular emotional responses (including love, respect, obedience, protection, and so on), and these, in turn, inspire trust. Due to its place within the cultural matrix and role in subject formation, motherhood evokes emotions that are extremely difficult to resist.

The god-term Mother (a rhetorical expression of the code of motherhood) is likewise imbued with cultural significance and pathetic force. UVVA rhetors' repeated references to the Mother permitted them to create emotional connections and establish trust with others, a foundation they then built upon by cultivating appeals from the motherhood topos. They exploited *kairic* opportunities arising from the murder of Laci Peterson and the trial of her husband, Scott; they employed language that cast the unborn as born children and implied that they, too, merited legal protection; they borrowed maternal ethos and authority from female survivors of violent crime; and they used images of the deceased to argue for the existence of two independent victims. MPA rhetors, on the other hand, had little rhetorical recourse to either the god term or the motherhood topos and used the opportunities they did have sparingly. Their inability either to refute UVVA speakers' maternal rhetorics or to discover an alternate cultural code capable of eliciting similar levels of emotion and trust contributed to the MPA's defeat. In the remainder of this section, I support these observations by analyzing congressional members' use of *kairos*, style, proof, and visual imagery, throughout charting their construction of pregnancy and its persuasive impact.

Kairos

Kairos concerns right timing: It entails evaluating the rhetorical elements of "place, speaker, and audience" and identifying propitious openings for shaping beliefs within a particular context (Helsley 371). A sensitivity to *kairos* and willingness to exploit it enabled UVVA proponents to resuscitate the two-victim crime bill after four previously unsuccessful runs through Congress. The Christmas Eve 2002 disappearance of Laci Peterson—young, white, middle-class, attractive, and eight-months pregnant—gave the bill sorely needed exigence. Peterson's distraught mother, Sharon Rocha, made frequent, impassioned pleas for her daughter's safe return to the media and coordinated a large, sustained search effort while Peterson's husband distanced himself from the press, appearing unconcerned and nonchalant. His curious demeanor, Rocha's visible distress, Peterson's vulnerability as a pregnant woman, and disclosure of Scott's extramarital affairs soon transformed a local missing-person case into a domestic drama of epic proportions that captivated the nation (see Crier). In April 2003, the bodies of a woman and fetus washed ashore in San Francisco Bay near the spot where Scott purportedly went fishing on the day of his wife's disappearance; soon after, he was arrested and charged with murdering Laci and the unborn Conner (Crier 355).

The Peterson case gave the UVVA a face and its proponents a *kairic* opportunity to revive the moribund bill. Republican members added *Laci and Conner's Law* to the bill's title in order to harness public interest and heighten awareness of inconsistent penalties for violence against pregnant women: "Under California law, [Scott] Peterson was convicted of murdering a 'person' and a 'fetus.' However, under the laws of other [state] jurisdictions, a similar crime could be prosecuted as the murders of two people or as one murder only" (Marzilli 9). Polls indicated that between 70 and 90 percent of respondents believed strongly that offenders should be held responsible for harm done to *both* a woman and her pregnancy (House H5, H40), sentiments that, in conjunction with media frenzy surrounding Scott Peterson's trial, hastened the UVVA's passage through Congress. In fact, jury selection was underway when the bill moved into the Senate in March 2004, an external event that added urgency to the proceedings.

Congressional members were keenly aware of the openings and expectations created by the Peterson case, as is suggested by their many references to it. Democrats tried to calm the situation, warning of the dangers of precipitous action. During House debate on 26 February

2004, for instance, Rep. Sheila Jackson-Lee complained that the impending trial was exerting undue pressure on Congress to respond quickly (House H645). Rep. Jan Schakowsky, in an attempt to defuse the imperative for immediate action, noted that the UVVA "would not even apply to the tragic Laci Peterson . . . [or] the vast majority of domestic violence cases," which were covered by state rather than federal law (House H642). Republicans, meanwhile, foregrounded the case and urged immediate modification of federal crime statutes. In the House alone, twenty UVVA supporters alluded to Laci and Conner's sad fate, no one more movingly than majority leader Tom DeLay, who was the final Republican speaker before representatives cast their votes for either the one- or two-victim crime bills.

Clearly cognizant of maternity's emotional resonance, DeLay portrayed Laci as a venerable Mother, defiled and discarded by the husband who *should* have protected her. Her murder violated common standards of decency that dictated respectful treatment of mothers in general and of pregnant women in particular. DeLay assumed listeners' shared reverence for motherhood and outrage at its violation, presumptions that threaded through a series of rhetorical questions: "Why are the attacks against pregnant women like Laci Peterson so egregious? Why should they merit harsher penalties? Why do all people in all cultures, naturally, instinctively, recoil at such attacks?" (House H666). His allusion to standards shared by "all people in all cultures, naturally, instinctively" suggested widespread agreement concerning the sanctity of motherhood. To explain why violence against expectant women was so offensive, however, the rhetor discussed pregnancy in terms of two subjects, not one: "It is the vulnerability of the pregnant mother, to be sure, but it is also the innocence and the very being of the unborn child" (House H666). Here, DeLay clinched his rhetorical set-up: Invoking the god-term Mother in his depiction of Laci and the cultural mandate to protect mothers created a moral imperative that he then extended to the unborn through a two-person figuration of pregnancy. He developed the theme by presenting Laci's "son" as an independent being and asserting the two-fold character of gestation:

> Laci Peterson had a son. He was never born, he never spoke a word or took his first steps, but he was real. Whoever killed Laci Peterson also killed her son, and to deny that is to deny truth. That unborn victims of violence are separate victims of violence is not a matter of interpretation, it is a matter of plain fact. A child could tell you that a man who kills a pregnant woman and her unborn child takes two lives. (House H665)

The speaker configured both the expectant woman and fetus as crime victims and argued that recognizing the loss of "two lives" was a simple matter of "truth," "plain fact," and "common sense." These doxa made DeLay's two-person paradigm of pregnancy seem timeless, self-evident, natural, and universal rather than rhetorically crafted and politically motivated.

After describing pregnancy as the cohabitation of two separate subjects in a single body, DeLay transitioned into the peroration and urged "civilized society" to "punish injustice, no matter the size, strength or political inconvenience of its victim" (House H666). In this manner, he opened a protective umbrella capacious enough to shelter expectant women *and* the unborn. He concluded that not only the secular realm but also the divine demanded acknowledgment of fetal personhood: "Laci Peterson's son may have been robbed from this world before he ever touched it, but . . . he was here. Today he may be looking down on us from the nurseries of Heaven, protected for eternity by the God who knit him together in the womb, nestled in the loving embrace of the mother who gave him his name, but before Conner Peterson was taken, . . . he was here" (House H666). DeLay insisted upon Conner's personhood and framed his death as a direct affront to God and society. He also suggested that the obligation to protect pregnant women and the unborn, when not embraced by husbands and fathers, fell to elected officials, who in this case might vindicate victims of violent crime by passing the UVVA in a timely fashion. Although he mentioned both Laci and Conner in his account of violated motherhood, DeLay's real interest was evidenced by 16 references to the unborn and only 6 to the pregnant woman within the space of 443 words, a proportion that is fairly typical in antiabortion discourse. Nevertheless, by beginning and ending with Laci's death, the rhetor exploited the persuasive possibilities afforded by a mother's murder and successfully argued for two-victim legislation.

The Peterson case, then, created a *kairic* opening that Republicans grasped in order to revive the UVVA, portray it as the right bill at the right time, and produce a sense of urgency regarding its passage. Furthermore, Laci's murder enabled UVVA proponents to highlight violations to the code of motherhood, stir communal outrage, and fan a collective desire for immediate action to remedy an egregious moral breach.

Style

The third canon, Paul Butler explains in *Out of Style: Reanimating Stylistic Study in Composition and Rhetoric*, concerns "the deployment of rhetorical resources . . . to create and express meaning," resources that include "conscious choices at the sentence and word level" regarding tone, emphasis, irony, vocabulary, diction, register, syntax, semantics, figures of speech, sound, and rhythm (2–3). Style, then, consists of far more than "mere ornamentation" and contributes substantially to meaning making, in part, through its capacity to convey emotion (146). The connections between style and emotion are examined in Book 3 of Aristotle's rhetorical treatise, which delineates the qualities and consequences of appropriate *lexis* (word choice or diction) in deliberative and forensic discourse. *Lexis* can make a person or subject matter seem "credible" and lead the mind to "a false inference of the truth" provided the speaker and audience "feel the same about such things"; words and emotion, properly combined, encourage listeners to "think the facts to be so, even if they are not as the speaker represents them" (3.7.4–5). Stated differently, fitting words elicit emotions and frame the world in ways that induce the audience to accept a rhetor and her truth claims.

To adapt these observations to congressional deliberation over the UVVA and MPA, members' paradigms of pregnancy and stance on reproductive choice shaped their rhetorical construction of motherhood and stylistic choices. Both sides adopted the established frameworks and lexicon of the abortion controversy. Advocates of the UVVA routinely referred to *mothers* or *expectant mothers* and to the *unborn child, child in utero, preborn child,* or *child waiting to be born,* language that simultaneously invoked the sanctity of motherhood and accorded "individual subjectivity and an aura of already-existing 'born personhood'" to the fetus (Stringer 9). Proponents of the MPA, meanwhile, alluded to *pregnant women* and the *embryo, fetus, pregnancy,* or *potential life,* terms that presented expectant women as subjects and withheld personhood status from the unborn. Congressional members' representations of pregnancy and lexical choices had very different outcomes in terms of creating pathos and garnering votes, as I explain below.

MPA proponents, through their framing and word choice, consistently forwarded a one-person paradigm of pregnancy and focused attention on female victims of violent crime. These moves were apparent, for example, in Sen. Feinstein's assessment of the MPA's and UVVA's imposition of penalties and implications for *Roe v Wade*. The one-victim MPA crime bill ensured that the perpetrator of an attack on a woman that either hurt or terminated her pregnancy could be charged, first, with "the underlying Federal crime" against her and, second, with "harming or killing another potential life" (Senate S3126). Feinstein prioritized women and their pregnancies and withheld personhood from the unborn by referring to *potential lives*. Arguing that the two bills' treatment of crime and imposition of penalties were the same, she identified their primary difference as "a few simple words that inject the abortion debate into this issue by clearly establishing in criminal law for the first time in history that life begins at the moment of conception. I contend that if this result is incorporated in law, it will be the first step in removing a woman's right to choice, particularly in the early months of a pregnancy before viability" (Senate S3126). Feinstein's truth claim regarding one-person pregnancy as well as her diction kept the spspotlight on women and made a sensible case for the MPA's superiority to the UVVA on the grounds that it preserved reproductive choice. Her remarks, however, were abstract and logos driven, concentrating on similarities and differences in the bills' penalties, definitions, and legal implications and disregarding emotional considerations almost entirely.

UVVA rhetors' two-person figuration of pregnancy permitted them to refer to *mothers* and *unborn children*, to access the emotional resonance of motherhood, and to make the consequences of violence concrete and compelling. These outcomes became apparent when Sen. Rick Santorum lambasted UVVA opponents' reluctance to inscribe "the humanity of the child" in law and fundamental misunderstanding of the bill's threat to *Roe*: "Who cares about what harm we may bring to a mother whose child is injured or what harm we may bring to the family who may lose or have an injury to a child in womb? Who cares that we cannot bring somebody who has done violence to a child in the womb to justice? All of those things are worth ignoring to protect this right [to reproductive choice] that is not even at stake today" (Senate S3136). Describing abortion as a "cancer" that was not only "eating away" at the "relationship between the mother and the child" but also infecting "areas that have nothing to do" with it, he implored colleagues "to let common sense reign in the Senate today" by respecting the personhood of the unborn victim of violence: "[T]his is a child who is loved and wanted by the mother. This is a child who, in many cases, has been given a name, such as Conner Peterson, and this is a child who deserves the dignity of recognition by our society" (Senate S3136). Santorum's primary concern was signaled by eight references to the unborn and only three to mothers. Motherhood, nevertheless, played an important role in his argument, enabling him to create pathos through references to mothers' love for "child[ren] in womb," to their affectionate naming practices (hence the mention of Conner Peterson), and to their grief upon losing pregnancies as a result of violence. Further, his word choice equated the relationship of a pregnant woman and fetus with that of a mother and born child, suggesting that if maternal love preceded nativity, then personhood began prior to birth as well. Santorum also invoked the code of motherhood: He drew upon the moral imperative to honor and protect expectant women and then, through the two-person construct of pregnancy, extended that protection to the unborn as well. Through these rhetorical choices, he brought shared scripts and codes into play, stirred emotion and encouraged trust, and set the stage for persuasion.

Speakers' references to a *mother* and *unborn child* or to a *woman* and *her pregnancy* impacted not only emotional tenor but also ethos. Miller notes that rhetors create socially legible character by upholding, modifying, or repudiating dominant codes and that those who fail to conform often run the risk of damaging their ethos (47). Because lexis reflects the cultural matrix, it, too, contributes to ethos formation. In this case, members whose word choice harmonized with the code of motherhood generally projected positive, trustworthy character while those who attempted to sidestep the code reaped shame and seemed heartless. These consequences were apparent, for instance, in Rep. Lofgren's remarks for and Rep. James Sensenbrenner's against the MPA. Sensenbrenner, who enjoyed full recourse to the motherhood topos, denounced the one-victim bill for "throw[ing] salt into the wounds" of female survivors of violent crime, women who were imploring Congress to acknowledge "the loss of their loved, unborn child": "These mothers are not seeking recognition of the violence they have suffered. They are seeking recognition of the violence their unborn children have suffered as well. They are seeking recognition of the loss of their unborn child" (House H661). In discussing pregnancy in terms of mothers and unborn children, the rhetor embraced the code of motherhood and projected good and compassionate character. As an added bonus, he harnessed the powerful emotions surrounding these figures and aligned himself with grieving survivors, garnering their trust.

Lofgren countered Sensenbrenner's argument calmly and rationally, noting that the MPA would actually impose tougher fines and sentencing penalties than the UVVA for "violent or assaultive conduct" against a woman that either interrupted or terminated her pregnancy (House H661). As was consonant with her political position, she used the expression *interrupting or terminating a pregnancy* to describe fetal loss, terminology that created serious ethical problems for her. Pro-choice advocates are frequently accused of being "inherently anti-children, anti-family, and anti-traditional women's roles," (mis)perceptions resulting, in part, from their reluctance to use words like *mother* and *child* to discuss pregnancy (Hull and Hoffer 4–5). Substituting *woman, fetus,* and *the unborn* for privileged maternal terms is often interpreted as disregard for or indifference to motherhood itself.

UVVA proponents were aware of their opponents' ethical vulnerability and regularly lambasted their impersonal diction, theoretical tone, and detached attitudes toward mothers and babies. Rep. Hart, for one, condemned the wording of the one-victim crime bill, which transformed the "death of the unborn child . . . into an abstraction, 'terminating a pregnancy'"; described "bodily injury inflicted upon the child" as "mere prenatal injury"; and labeled such loss as an "interruption of the normal course of pregnancy" (House H663). "These abstractions," she complained, ignored "the fact that the death of the unborn child occurs when a pregnancy is violently terminated by a criminal" and that "a prenatal injury is an injury inflicted upon a human being in the womb of his or her mother" (House H663). Hart, in effect, charged MPA supporters with being as cold and clinical as their language and, therefore, unconcerned with prenatal deaths due to violence. Her critique of the bill also implied that its advocates flouted the cultural mandate to protect *mothers* (and, by extension, their *unborn children*). In effect, she positioned MPA proponents away from the Mother and toward the Woman end of the rhetorical continuum, marking them as deviant and hurting their ethos.

The emotional and ethical impact of *lexis*, then, can be profound. Hart and Sensenbrenner's two-person paradigm of pregnancy and truth claims for the fetus as always/already a legal subject gave them access to the topos, code, and god term associated with motherhood, rhetorical resources unavailable to those who identified live birth as the beginning of personhood. As the examples above suggest, references to *mothers, unborn children,* and *human beings in the womb* were far more affective than those to *women, pregnancies,* and *potential lives*. Congressional members' stances and frameworks, claims and objectives, constrained their stylistic choices and gave UVVA supporters more evocative language and credible ethos than MPA proponents. These advantages contributed greatly to passage of the two-victim crime bill.

Proofs

Congressional members integrated witness accounts, data, expert opinion, and gendered bodies into their presentations in order to shore up their respective positions. UVVA supporters relied heavily upon testimony from survivors of violent crime, including Sharon Rocha, Carol Lyons, Shiwona Pace, and Tracy Marciniak, all of whom had detailed their painful experiences at preliminary committee hearings and urged passage of two-victim legislation. Rep. John Lewis, for example, quoted the bereaved mother of pregnant murder-victim Ashley Lyons (and grandmother of the unborn Landon) on the House floor: "Nobody can tell me that there were not two victims. I placed Landon in Ashley's arms, wrapped in a baby blanket that I had sewn for him, just before I kissed my daughter goodbye for the last time and closed the casket" (House H644–45). In a similar vein, Rep. Mike Pence repeated Rocha's plea for Laci and Conner's Law:

> A single-victim amendment would be a painful blow to those, like me, who are left alive after a two-victim crime, because Congress would be saying that Conner and other innocent unborn victims like him are not really victims, indeed, that they never really existed at all. But our grandson did live. He had a name, he was loved, and his life was violently taken from him before he ever saw the sun. (House H645)

As Lewis and Pence's incorporation of these passages suggests, survivors communicated their abiding grief and anger forcefully and made a compelling case for recognizing two, rather than one, victims of violent crime. Their voices added authority and credibility to pro-UVVA arguments and gave proponents the good reasons and poignant emotions needed to promote two-victim legislation. Furthermore, because most of the survivors were mothers, members were able to "borrow" maternal ethos through citation, a move that was particularly helpful to UVVA supporters, most of whom were men. To illustrate with the roster of House speakers, Sensenbrenner made the group's opening remarks (later speaking from the floor as needed) and was followed by Steve Chabot, Melissa Hart, Pete King, Phil Gingrey, Cliff Stearns, John Lewis, Scott Garrett, Mike Pence, Robert Aderholt, Patrick Kennedy, Ginny Brown-Waite, Roscoe Bartlett, Mike Ferguson, and Henry Hyde (House H654–60). In all, thirteen men and two women spoke for the bill. UVVA proponents compensated for a predominantly male lineup by weaving female survivors' testimony into their remarks, in that way incorporating mothers' voices and aligning women with their bill.

Meanwhile, MPA speakers integrated testimony chiefly to demonstrate the extent of opposition to the UVVA and "lift the veil" concerning its antiabortion agenda. In her opening remarks alone, Sen. Feinstein cited an editorial from the *Philadelphia Enquirer*, three law professors, and Justice Harry Blackmun to establish the threat that two-victim legislation posed to *Roe v. Wade*. She also quoted four UVVA supporters who stated candidly that legally encoding fetal personhood, as the bill would do, represented an important step toward overturning the Supreme Court decision (Senate S3125–28). Feinstein's use of testimony shed light on the long-term dangers that two-victim legislation posed to women's reproductive rights and alarmed those committed to preserving them.

Some MPA proponents highlighted maternity and shared their personal histories, in effect, serving as witnesses themselves. Rep. Schakowsky, for instance, countered accusations that MPA supporters did "not care about women" or "the babies that they [carry]" by announcing that she was both a mother and a grandmother and expressing concern for women, their pregnancies, and their children (House H642). She also introduced her own maternal experience in order to promote one-victim legislation: The MPA "recognizes that the pregnant woman is a victim when she is assaulted, instead of making the fetus distinct and separate from the woman, which anybody who is pregnant or has been pregnant knows is really not [the case] when you are carrying that child." Schakowsky argued that her bill, unlike the UVVA, got "to the heart of the matter: protecting pregnant women from violence" (House H642). Incorporating women's felt sense in this manner, in effect, created insider/outsider positions, suggesting that only those with first-hand knowledge of pregnancy were qualified to choose appropriate penalties for harming or ending one. Schakowsky, thus, drew upon the authority and corporeal perceptions of motherhood to create ethical and logical appeals.

MPA proponent Zoe Lofgren also incorporated maternal history, relating her heartache at a failed pregnancy: "Those of us who have experienced a miscarriage understand a very essential truth: The loss is something you never forget. Whether the woman is 6 weeks pregnant or 6 months pregnant, the loss is acutely felt by that woman, and it deserves the full penalty that the law can provide" (House H661). Addressing her miscarriage contributed positively to Lofgren's ethos, demonstrating good sense grounded in experience and good will toward those who likewise grieved a pregnancy; her brief statement, however, was the most she made of the persuasive possibilities of motherhood. Lofgren's fleeting allusion to miscarriage in the House was, in fact, far less personal, detailed, and compelling than her earlier remarks to the House Committee of the Judiciary, which considered the UVVA prior to its reintroduction to Congress:

> All of us here on the Committee have had exciting moments and some fame or notoriety, but I have got to tell you that the absolute most exciting moment of my entire life was when I gave birth to my children. And it is a moment that . . . I can remember as if it was yesterday. It is one of the most enriching and exciting experiences of one's life. And for anyone who has had a miscarriage, as I have had, you know the disappointment, really the devastation that comes with that loss. There is nothing really larger than to lose a pregnancy and to not have the child that you thought you would have. It is something that you really never get over. But when that is something that really comes from the hand of God rather than the hand of an assault, you make your peace with it. To imagine that that loss would be caused by the violence of another is really unbelievable and really deserves the very largest penalty that we can possibly devise, because to deny a woman the opportunity to have her much desired child is a lifelong sentence. And those who would assault someone and cause a miscarriage, they deserve a life sentence, in my judgment, for the harm that they have done. (Committee 47)

Lofgren described the elation and devastation, the reward and grief of pregnancy, childbirth, miscarriage, and motherhood in this statement. In recounting her experience and emotions, she created vivid, affecting discourse and authoritative ethos. Finally, she yoked the material to promoting more stringent sentencing penalties for violence against pregnant women. Although similar details and appeals might have been incorporated into her House remarks, they were used minimally by the rhetor. Why? Did Lofgren, as a woman and member of an underrepresented group, feel ill at ease or vulnerable sharing information of an intimate nature with male colleagues? Women, after all, comprised only 14 percent of the House in 2004 (60 of 435 members) and so were clearly marked and outnumbered (Center 2). Did she fear that maternal testimony would be interpreted negatively as "playing the gender card"? Or was she (and other pro-choice speakers) constrained by a one-person paradigm of pregnancy that compelled her to emphasize women rather mothers? In such a case, invoking motherhood, which necessarily entails children, might have seemed a risky or inconsistent persuasive move. Regardless, Lofgren's reluctance to embrace maternal rhetorics at her disposal marked a missed opportunity to harness powerful emotions and connotations to her bill.

Although MPA proponents generally eschewed maternal appeals, they employed gender astutely in other ways during House debate. To illustrate, following the UVVA's introduction, Rep. Nadler glossed his and his colleagues' objections to the bill (he subsequently retook the floor as needed); he was, then, followed by a full roster of women rhetors who expanded upon its weaknesses: Nita Lowey, Jan Schakowsky, Sheila Jackson-Lee, Carolyn Maloney, Hilda Solis, Tammy Baldwin, Lynn Woolsey, and Diane Watson. Male representatives entered written opposition to the UVVA into the record so as to avoid diluting the lineup of women speakers (see House H654–60). Additionally, after discussion of the UVVA ended, Lofgren introduced the alternate MPA and was, in turn, followed by Lynn Woolsey, Tammy Baldwin, Eleanor Norton, Loretta Sanchez, and Diana DeGette. Again, male colleagues entered written support into the record as a procession of female representatives argued for legislation designed to protect pregnant women from harm while also preserving their reproductive rights. Throughout, the rhetors' gendered bodies bore silent witness to their authority to speak on the subject.

Congressional members on both sides of the aisle, then, wove a variety of rhetorical proofs into their remarks but with different aims and results. Given their goal of protecting reproductive choice, MPA supporters incorporated expert opinion in order to uncover the antiabortion agenda and legal implications of two-victim legislation, a tactic that depended chiefly upon logos. And even though they largely avoided the motherhood topos , MPA rhetors' embodied performance of gender, which might be framed as corporeal evidence, greatly enhanced their ethos. Meanwhile, the primarily male proponents of the UVVA relied heavily upon the testimony of female survivors of violent crime, who constructed pregnancy as a two-person condition and shared harrowing accounts of love, betrayal, and loss. Integrating survivors' remarks into House and Senate debate enabled UVVA supporters to borrow maternal ethos, appropriate the strong emotions associated with motherhood, and make women's arguments for two-victim legislation audible within the political forum.

Visuals

Photographs are rhetorical representations of the world, shaped through framing, cropping, and lighting and manipulated digitally and in the darkroom. However, they are often accepted uncritically as faithful reproductions of reality and truthful reflections of the world. Assumptions regarding photography's transparency, realism, and objectivity explain why it is so often embraced as undisputable "evidence of an object's existence," even within deliberative and forensic settings (Chandler 43). UVVA rhetors employed photographs shrewdly to this end, translating abstract controversies about crime and punishment into specific mothers and unborn children and using images of their bodies to advance partisan "truths" about pregnancy, personhood, and policy.

To support these observations, I turn to a photograph that was presented during committee hearings on the UVVA by Tracy Marciniak, a survivor whose advocacy of two-victim legislation was fueled by abiding heartache and fury at loopholes in Wisconsin law. Marciniak was severely beaten by her husband five days prior to her due date and, in consequence, miscarried; her assailant, however, was charged only with assault because "in the eyes of the law, no one died" (Brownback, Senate S3143). To demonstrate the extent of her loss, she shared a photograph taken at the funeral of her unborn child, Zachariah (which can be viewed at http://www.nrlc.org/Unborn_Victims/Zachariah.jpg). It showed Marciniak cradling and gazing down at what appeared to be a sleeping newborn. The profound sadness on the mother's face and viewers' dawning realization that the infant she held would never awake unleashed a torrent of strong feelings, including sympathy for Marciniak, anger at her abuser, and outrage at the violated cultural mandate to protect pregnant women. Emotional responses to visual images, according to Robert Hariman and John Louis Lucaites, are intensified when those depicted seem innocent and vulnerable, as was certainly the case with the bereaved mother and deceased child (42). UVVA rhetors were sensitive not only to the funeral photograph's poignancy but also to the visual support it provided for their two-person construct of pregnancy.

Images, of course, do not simply disclose their significance to viewers. Roland Barthes observes that verbal messages anchor photographic meaning in two ways, through identification and through interpretation. When viewers "hesitate" to decode a photograph's "forms and masses," words can steer them to "the correct level of perception" by focusing their "gaze" and their "understanding" (Barthes, "Rhetoric" 39). Before the Marciniak picture could provide UVVA proponents with persuasive means, the figures within it (and their relationship to each other) had to be identified; Rep. Sensenbrenner made these moves when he unveiled the photograph during opening remarks to the House:

> Tracy Marciniak, whose unborn child was murdered by her husband, has told Congress, "Please don't tell me that my son was not a murder victim." The Unborn Victims of Violence Act, I hope, will pass this body overwhelmingly today if only each Member opens their eyes to the photo of the dead body of Tracy Marciniak's murdered child and opens their hearts to the mothers who have implored Congress to give their unborn babies the status they deserve under the criminal law. (House H639)

Sensenbrenner clarified the image's initial ambiguity, identifying a "mother" holding the "dead body" of her "murdered child," and, in so doing, set the stage for mining its deeper significance. Interpretation, according to Barthes, plays a vital role in unraveling a photograph's "symbolic message," acting as "a kind of vice" that prevents potential readings from becoming too idiosyncratic or from "proliferating" endlessly ("Rhetoric" 39). Sensenbrenner interpreted Marciniak's and Zachary's bodies as visual proof that two independent persons coexisted during pregnancy. Of course, to make that argument, he had to gloss over the fact that one never lived outside the womb, an omission belied by his conflation of the born and the unborn in descriptions of Zachariah as a "baby," "son," "child," and "victim." Sensenbrenner's verbal identification and interpretation of the image anchored a two-person paradigm of pregnancy and made a material, if fallacious, case for the late-term fetus as a rights-bearing subject. As Jay Dolmage and Cynthia Lewiecki-Wilson so wisely caution, it is important to attend to "the logic of the visual" as visual logic is not necessarily sound logic (32).

UVVA proponents consistently argued that the Marciniak photograph revealed "the deeper 'essence' of what it depict[ed]," its two figures disclosing the real nature of pregnancy and personhood. The picture's purported "visual truth," in other words, was equated to an "abstract truth" (Van Leeuwen 168). This strategy undergirded Rep. Steve Chabot's assertion that the funeral image encapsulated the two crime bills' central point of contention: "This entire debate is best summed up in a single photograph. Whether or not there are two victims in this photograph or only one is the issue that is at hand" (House H662–63). UVVA supporters counted the number of bodies in the Marciniak photograph and interpreted each as a separate legal entity. In this manner, the "visual truth" of the image was made to support a highly partisan "abstract truth" about personhood. Other representatives employed and extended the body-count argument to urge passage of two-victim legislation. Rep. Mike Ferguson, for example, showed the House a photograph of Ashley Lyons (who was murdered alongside her fetus) and asked, "Did two people die when Ashley Lyons and her son, Landon, were murdered, or just one? Was a murder committed when Tracy Marciniak was beaten and her unborn son was killed? During the search for Laci Peterson and her unborn son, Conner, in San Francisco, did they find two bodies or did they find just one body?" (House H649). Enumerating the literal, figurative, and photographic forms of women and the unborn, Ferguson interpreted each body as a separate victim. Granted, rhetorical sleight of hand was needed to discuss each pregnancy in terms of two independent persons, for Landon, Zachariah, and Conner all expired in the womb. The visceral emotion and graphic power of victim photographs, however, enabled UVVA rhetors to mask logical inconsistencies and make a compelling case for their bill.

In contrast, supporters of the one-victim crime bill had little recourse to visual rhetoric. Furthermore, when they challenged UVVA speakers' interpretations of funeral photographs, MPA proponents risked seeming "callous to the emotional pull of fetal images and extreme in their preference for women's rights over fetal rights" (Casey 14). Their ethos was placed in jeopardy. Sen. Feinstein negotiated the dilemma by confessing the difficulty of responding to the "litany of atrocities" detailed by UVVA advocates and acknowledging both the reprehensibility of the crimes and her empathy for survivors: "I understand the need to . . . punish, and understand the need . . . to say [that] this child—who is so close to birth, who would be capable of life outside of the womb at that moment—is a victim because, in fact, that child is a victim" (Senate S3144). Feinstein's lexical slippage, describing the unborn as a child and awarding it victim status, revealed the enormity of her challenge. That concession, however, also helped her to establish good will and good moral character, after which she tackled fallacies in her colleagues' visual and verbal arguments for two-victim legislation:

Every single case presented on this Senate floor this morning is of a child who is viable outside of the womb. But the bill covers children that are not children; that are a day old in the womb, that are at conception. That is the problem we have with this bill. Because once you give an embryo, at the point of conception, all of the legal rights of a human being, . . . [you have] created the legal case to go against Roe v. Wade in Federal law for the first time in history. (Senate S3144)

Even as she conceded the humanity of the viable, full-term fetus, Feinstein maintained that the UVVA was bad legislation, noting its failure to distinguish among different stages of development and its long-term implications for reproductive choice. However, she did not manage either to defuse the emotions generated by survivor photographs or to create equally compelling pathetic appeals of her own, a problem that plagued MPA supporters throughout congressional deliberation.

In this section, I have examined politicians' construction of pregnancy, recourse to maternal rhetorics, and overall persuasiveness. Depending upon their stance on abortion and personhood, rhetors depicted pregnancy as involving either one or two subjects, and these paradigms, in turn, produced very different persuasive affordances and constraints. UVVA speakers' contention that the unborn was always/already a person prompted an emphasis on mothers and children and gave them full access to the code, topos, and god term associated with motherhood. In consequence, they were able to deploy dominant cultural scripts, invoke communal precepts and feelings, and appear credible and trustworthy. Meanwhile, MPA speakers recognized live birth as the beginning of personhood and focused chiefly on women's rights; they generally refrained from using motherhood rhetorically but failed to discover a powerful alternative to it. As a result, MPA discourse sounded sensible, sterile, and flat while UVVA discourse bloomed with color and passion. Speakers' paradigms of pregnancy, recourse to motherhood, and strategic use of *kairos*, *lexis*, proofs, and visuals ultimately spelled either victory or defeat for their crime bills.

The House of Representatives approved the UVVA on 26 February 2004 by a vote of 254 to 163, and the Senate followed suit on 25 March 2004 with a vote of 61 to 38 (House H667–68; Senate S3167).[7] The act added a federal component to the growing body of state feticide laws currently on a collision course with *Roe v Wade*. It also was symbolically significant.

Congress is one of the most important lawmaking bodies in the nation; therefore, its passage of the UVVA further normalizes the concept of fetal personhood and is certain to influence future legislation and court decisions involving the unborn.

—

Personhood is determined through a complex series of rhetorical negotiations that have serious ramifications for women's legal, political, and reproductive rights. This chapter's examination of congressional deliberation over the UVVA is more broadly relevant, for it reflects ongoing debates about abortion within U.S. public discourse. What insights emerge from considering Laci and Conner's Law? First, the pro-choice movement must either embrace changing constructs of pregnancy or else identify new and more effective ways to counteract them. UVVA supporters' two-person paradigm of pregnancy and consequent use of maternal rhetorics played important roles in the bill's passage and fetal personhood's entry into federal law. MPA rhetors' one-person construct of pregnancy kept their focus strictly on expectant women and afforded few options for countering appeals that highlighted vulnerable mothers and innocent (unborn) children. Lacking equally compelling rhetorical means, MPA rhetors were reactive, endlessly detailing the long-term threat of two-victim legislation for *Roe v Wade* rather than building a moving and memorable case for their own bill.

Until the pro-choice movement reconsiders its one-person paradigm of pregnancy and comes to terms with the public fetus, it will continue to produce ineffective discourse and to hemorrhage its base of support. As the intensifying War on Women indicates, it is imperative to devise new rhetorical strategies capable of protecting women's fragile reproductive freedoms. One possibility is to expand the construct of pregnancy sufficiently to acknowledge the unique status of the viable, late-term fetus. Indeed, some pro-choice advocates believe the movement cannot succeed in the present social and political climate unless it modifies its hard-line stance, a thesis that is thoughtfully presented in Frances Kissling's provocative essay "Is There Life after *Roe*? How to Think about the Fetus." Written in response to the UVVA debacle, Kissling laments the extreme positions assumed by both sides of the abortion controversy, stances that have required each to promote problematic and, at times, absurd arguments. Pro-choice supporters, for instance, have been obliged to oppose the regulation of abortion at any stage of pregnancy and to defend late-term abortion; pro-life supporters have felt compelled to deny any "distinction in fetal value at any stage in pregnancy" and to challenge abortion in all cases, making no exceptions for rape and incest (190–91). Such extremism has discouraged "the development of an abortion praxis that combine[s] respect for the fundamental right of women to choose abortion with an ethical discourse that include[s] the exploration of how other values might also be respected, including the value of developing human life" (191). The pro-choice movement has lost popular support due to its refusal to consider the question of fetal value or how it might be recognized without imperiling legal abortion. Kissling suggests it is time to craft an ethical pro-choice platform that pursues the middle way. However, before the movement can undertake that effort, it must revisit the one-person construct of pregnancy. Granted, modifying that paradigm might well lead to an extremely slippery slope, but it might also open up new options for negotiating female and fetal rights at different stages of the gestational process. A willingness to wrestle with the complexities and moral ambiguities of pregnancy and abortion may be essential to (re)winning the backing of a broad constituency of Americans, many of whom have been alienated by the movement's intractability. (For an insightful pro-choice counterargument to Kissling, see Rebecca Traister's "Morality Play.")

Changing the rhetorical playing field of the abortion controversy may also require new legal tactics. For one, the pro-choice movement may need to pick its battles more carefully. It contested the UVVA due to the bill's long-term threat to *Roe v Wade*. However, because abortion was specifically exempted by the bill, opposition made pro-choicers look like "callous" and "extreme ideological zealots," seriously damaging movement ethos (Young, n.p.). The antiabortion movement has demonstrated the wisdom of choosing the right battles and changing legal strategy when necessary. Its decision to lobby for fetal personhood only in situations that do not directly threaten women's reproductive choice, for example, has paid handsome dividends (Saletan 233). That particular locus makes it is possible to align, rather than oppose, female and fetal interests, a far easier position from which to argue. The tactic's success is evident in the plethora of new state and federal laws that frame both women and the unborn as crime victims and create precedent for challenging *Roe*. Pro-choice proponents might, likewise, benefit from identifying loci that enable them to recognize the unique status of the late-term fetus and to concentrate on protecting abortion prior to viability.

In addition to revised legal strategy, a new lexicon and framework are called for as well. The antiabortion movement has claimed "the vocabulary of life and loss" as its own, making the "ability to move" others the most notable feature of its discourse (Traister 228; Hayden, "Revitalizing" 124). Pro-choice rhetors must reclaim "language that is emotional, conciliatory, moralistic, and even religious" in order to put "the heart back into the fight for abortion rights" and "warm up what has come to be regarded as an absolutist, clinical, chilly movement" (Traister 228). Such change necessitates developing a lexicon that evokes feeling and identifying new approaches. According to Sarah Hayden, foregrounding the harm and benefits of proposed legislation not only to women but also to their children and families may provide the movement with a more expansive framework, capable of generating emotion and inviting identification ("Revitalizing" 124).

Modifying its language and paradigm of pregnancy might also give the pro-choice movement recourse to rhetorics of motherhood. Invoking powerful cultural codes, creating connections with others, and stimulating trust and feelings are missing elements in current pro-choice discourse. Appropriating motherhood might also help to repair damaged movement ethos and attract new (or alienated) audiences to the cause. Softening the movement's stance on pregnancy and fetal value, then, may prove key to accessing the code, topos, and terms of motherhood; to uncovering cultural and emotional grounds for attracting and retaining adherents; to developing new formulas for balancing the rights of women and the unborn at different stages of gestation; and to protecting abortion prior to viability. Such concessions are risky, but as the stakes surrounding the abortion controversy escalate, so, too, do the political, legal, social, and ethical consequences of arguing effectively for women's reproductive control.

Conclusion:
Interrogating Motherhood, Transforming Gender

> Certainly it is possible to theorize women's situations and expe-
> riences, or to theorize gender, in ways that minimize the issue
> of mothering, or do not address it at all. But assumptions about
> women's mothering are so deeply embedded in U.S. society and
> culture and are so complexly intertwined with other funda-
> mental beliefs and values that these assumptions are likely to be
> implicit in accounts of women's situations and experiences and
> in theories of gender that do not explicitly address mothering.
> —Patrice DiQuinzio, *The Impossibility of Motherhood*

Those who study women but ignore motherhood do so at some peril, for, as Patrice DiQuinzio observes, it permeates culture, society, and politics. Although motherhood is both powerful and pervasive, its construction and implications for women have been little studied within rhetoric to this point. *Rhetorics of Motherhood* represents my effort to encourage scholarly conversation on the topic as well as the integration of women and women's issues into disciplinary histories, theories, and traditions.

I have assumed that socially constructed "categories have meaning and consequences," fostering both hierarchies and inequities (Crenshaw 1297), and have argued that the god-term Mother and devil-term Woman operate as poles on a continuum that affords rhetors means for praising or blaming women, practices, and policies. I employed this continuum in three case studies, exploring motherhood's Janus-like capacity not only to position women advantageously but also to constrain them. I also examined motherhood's versatility as a rhetorical resource, one that generates persuasive means useful for advocating feminist, resistant, and conservative agendas. Margaret Sanger's appropriation of motherhood to repair damaged ethos, appeal to diverse audiences, develop a large-scale movement for birth control, and, ultimately, increase women's reproductive self-determination illustrated a feminist application.[1] Meanwhile, Diane Nash employed maternal appeals to critique southern justice and exhort civil-rights cohorts to embrace jail-no-bail policy, thereby resisting racist power structures and promoting desegregation through nonviolent means. Finally, as congressional deliberation over The Unborn Victims of Violence Act (UVVA) revealed, maternal rhetorics proved central in advancing regressive politics and policies. UVVA speakers' two-person construct of pregnancy and invocation of the god term ensured passage of conservative legislation that, ironically, undermined women's control over when and whether to become mothers. These studies illuminated rhetors' use of motherhood to oppose, modify, or preserve the status quo, in each case drawing upon the Woman/ Mother continuum and shaping women's legal, social, political, and professional standing.

In these closing pages, I offer some final reflections on motherhood and public discourse, gleaned from bringing the Sanger, Nash, and UVVA chapters into relationship with one another. Specifically, I consider motherhood's cultural entrenchment and the emotional consequences of that placement; its ethical promise and peril for women; its influence on their rhetorical practices and careers; its usefulness for praising and/or blaming women; and its contingency and ever evolving meaning.

Culture, Code, and Emotion

Motherhood's persuasive force stems from its place in the cultural matrix. Embedded within an overarching system of gender, motherhood reflects prevailing beliefs about sex and sexuality, femininity and masculinity, reproduction and children. These beliefs permeate the code of motherhood, a mélange of the precepts, values, expectations, and conventions about maternity that support the gendered status quo. The code, in turn, is part of the comprehensive body of scripts, norms, and roles learned by subjects during the process of acculturation, so it is instantly recognizable to cultural insiders. The code of motherhood, therefore, provides rhetors with invaluable opportunities to bond "with audiences by deploying what everyone knows" (Miller 67). This positioning also accounts for motherhood's ability to stir strong emotion. Mention the code, and a series of mandates comes immediately to mind (say, the imperatives to protect pregnant women or to concede authority over home and children to mothers). Honoring or violating these mandates, in turn, evokes inculcated emotional responses: Those who harm, rather than protect, mothers and children, for instance, inspire outrage. The code's well-known standards and affiliated emotions imbue motherhood with enormous force and significance.

The god-term Mother is a rhetorical expression of the code of motherhood. Rhetors who invoke the god term slot audience members into familiar subject positions and encourage established emotional responses, ranging from respect and allegiance to anger and fear. The audience's immediate recognition of and reaction to the Mother is dictated by the *sensus communis*, enabling the rhetor to create common ground, provoke feeling, and inspire trust (see Miller). These moves typically transpire below the level of conscious awareness and permit speakers to prepare the ground for persuasion quickly and quietly. Further, because the Mother is recognized by and meaningful to everyone, it is particularly useful for addressing and connecting to diverse audiences. Its social centrality explains why the Mother is easy to introduce but difficult to resist or refute within public discourse.

Motherhood's emotional tenor and persuasive impact were readily apparent in both the Sanger and UVVA chapters. Sanger's bereavement following her daughter's death inspired an outpouring of sympathy and support, a response that awakened her appreciation for motherhood's ability to move those schooled to its code. She subsequently emphasized her maternal status in order to connect emotionally with others, establish trust, and encourage affiliation. By aligning herself and her cause with the Mother, Sanger created common ground with other women and inspired action on behalf on other mothers. Her sensitivity to motherhood's place within the cultural matrix, its emotional qualities, and its widespread appeal contributed greatly to her efforts to cultivate the birth-control movement. Along similar lines, UVVA proponents stressed the code of motherhood's mandate to protect pregnant women and highlighted its breach by perpetrators of violent crime. In naming their bill after Laci and Conner Peterson, they not only stimulated outrage at the abuse of a vulnerable *mother* and *unborn child* but also gained stature through their efforts to uphold the code (belatedly) and exact retribution. UVVA rhetors tapped into deep reservoirs of prescribed feelings about mothers and motherhood, which enabled them to craft strong appeals and ensured passage of two-victim legislation. Both case studies indicate that motherhood's persuasive energy stems from the code's pivotal place within the gender system and the Mother's symbolic and emotional resonance with cultural insiders.

Ethos: Substitution and Erasure

Maternal ethos is typically simple and straightforward, transforming a complex, multifaceted woman into a familiar, reassuring character. This flattening effect derives from motherhood's affiliation with dominant social, historical, and ideological constructs of gender, which the code presents as natural, eternal, and inevitable. Gender's "contingent foundations" are thereby converted into "Common Sense, Right Reason, the Norm, General Opinion, in short the *doxa*" (Barthes, "Change the Object Itself" 165). Because motherhood transmits gendered *doxa* in a relatively untroubled and uncontested fashion, maternal ethos communicates conformity to and affiliation with the powers that be.

Motherhood's conservatism can be a boon to women rhetors. As I noted in regard to Sanger, maternal ethos camouflaged her feminist objectives and controversial background as a socialist and revolutionary. Her ethos as a mother, in other words, subsumed her identity as a radical and feminist. Roland Barthes's insights into connotation and denotation illuminate motherhood's contributions to Sanger's formation of public character. In chapter 1, I reviewed Barthes's analysis of a *Paris Match* cover and his distinction between first- and second-order signification, the former denoting a "black soldier . . . giving the French salute" and the latter extending and complicating that meaning through connotations of "Frenchness" and "militariness" (*Mythologies* 118). Similarly, Sanger's ethical invocation of motherhood elicited a connotative complex of gendered *doxa* that, like the soldier's "Frenchness" and "militariness," were well known and comforting to audiences. At the level of second-order signification, the Mother engulfed Sanger, the specific woman, erasing her questionable past and promoting a socially sanctioned character in its place. Sanger projected maternal ethos and then hid in plain sight behind the Mother. The rhetor's success in reformulating her and her movement's ethe suggests that the god term's tendency to disguise and supplant is desirable and advantageous in certain situations.

However, motherhood's propensity to promote cultural stereotypes can also have detrimental consequences. In Nash's case, it contributed to her commemoration as a mother, rather than a leader, in histories of the civil-rights movement. She employed maternal appeals brilliantly, if briefly, to explain her appeal revocation and decision to enter jail while pregnant; subsequent accounts of the event focused almost exclusively on Nash's impending motherhood, in effect promoting maternal ethos at the expense of her logical and organizational acumen. Barthes's observations again shed light upon the Mother's displacement of the activist. Connotative form, he remarked, does not entirely suppress denotative (or literal) meaning but instead impoverishes it. Therefore, although the soldier on the cover of *Paris Match* endured as "a rich, fully experienced, spontaneous, innocent, *indisputable* image," it was simultaneously "tamed, put at a distance, made almost transparent" by connotations of French imperialism (Barthes, *Mythologies* 118). In like manner, historians' unrelenting attention to Nash's pregnancy summoned the god-term Mother, which in ethical terms subdued the woman of color, rhetor, and movement leader. Maternal ethos diminished Nash the strategist and commemorated a courageous Mother in her place.

In the cases of both Sanger and Nash, the god term displaced the woman with very different consequences. Maternal ethos smoothed out Sanger's potentially troubling past but overwhelmed Nash's leadership, contributing to her historical marginalization. These distinct outcomes suggest the mutability and Janus-like quality of motherhood in public discourse, revealing its dual capacity to benefit and undermine women.

Rhetorical Practice

The code of motherhood reinforces gendered doxa and exerts pressure on women across differences of identity and social location. One of its long-standing tenets holds that a mother's place is at home with her children, an expectation that creates real challenges for women in public life. As I detail in *Regendering Delivery: The Fifth Canon and Antebellum Women Rhetors*, motherhood has frequently had an adverse impact on women's careers, halting, interrupting, or postponing them (121–29). Maternal rhetors have, nevertheless, developed ingenious strategies for accommodating conflicting domestic and civic obligations. One popular and effective method is collaboration, a cooperative endeavor involving two or more people that results in a rhetorical product, performance, or event (134). While credit for the outcome may go either to an individual or a collective, the rhetorical artifact itself is constructed and completed through the direct and/or indirect assistance of others.

Collaboration was integral to the rhetorical practices of both Nash and Sanger after they became mothers. Although Nash for the most part relinquished direct public participation following the birth of her children, retirement did not end her contributions to the civil-rights movement. Indeed, her ongoing involvement was likely fueled by the African-American tradition of *community othermothering*, which encouraged women to attend simultaneously to raising their families and to ensuring broader "group survival, empowerment, and identity" (Collins, "Shifting" 58–59; Collins, *Black Feminist Thought* 189–92). In collaboration with her husband, James Bevel, Nash continued to plan major civil-rights initiatives, including the 1963 Birmingham desegregation campaign, the 1963 March on Washington for Jobs and Freedom, and the 1965 Selma voting-rights campaign ("Nash," n.p.). Although she occasionally pitched ideas to movement leaders, she more often remained at home with the children while Bevel presented and coordinated their projects in the field. The Nash/Bevel partnership constituted what I call *productive collaboration*, whereby two or more people contribute *directly* to the crafting and completion of such rhetorical products as campaigns, addresses, or public events (Buchanan, *Regendering* 134). Productive collaboration made it possible for Nash to sustain her engagement with the movement, but Bevel, not she, received most of the credit for their work, an attribution that contributed to her marginalization within civil-rights history. Nash's predicament illustrates how maternal pressures and expectations can shape women's rhetorical praxis and public recognition.

Sanger also collaborated extensively with others, but hers was often supportive, rather than productive, in nature. In *supportive collaborations*, one person's efforts contribute *indirectly* to another's discursive production and delivery, a form of assistance that is indispensable to maternal rhetors. Families caring for children, hired help supervising households, coworkers shouldering business responsibilities, supporters contributing financial resources, institutions providing children with shelter or care: These indirect and frequently overlooked types of collaboration enable women to meet domestic and maternal obligations while sustaining rhetorical engagements in the public sphere (Buchanan, *Regendering* 135). Sanger benefited greatly from supportive collaborations with friends, family, admirers, and institutions over the years. To illustrate, separation from her husband and commitment to radical action led to prolonged periods apart from her children. Although such absences violated the code of motherhood, they were, in fact, common among single and working mothers in the early twentieth century: "Employed women of all classes often solved child-care problems," Linda Gordon observes, by placing children temporarily in institutions (either orphanages or schools), with relatives, or with foster parents (*Dorothea* 109). Sanger followed this course when she fled the country in response to *Woman Rebel* charges and lived abroad for a year. During that period, her sister Ethel Byrne assumed primary responsibility for the three Sanger children (Katz 134–36) while the financial contributions of friends and supporters covered the costs of summer camps and boarding schools, institutional resources that enabled the rhetor to stay abroad and educate herself on the issue of birth control. Supportive collaboration, thus, provided the children with proper care and the mother with invaluable time and freedom.

Despite the vision of domestic motherhood promoted by the code, Nash's and Sanger's continued public involvement following childbirth exemplifies women's resourcefulness in overcoming gender constraints. Their collaborative relationships also link them to a long line of women rhetors, whose cooperative partnerships likewise permitted them to negotiate conflicting maternal and civic interests, to access public forums, and to produce and deliver discourse. Reliance on supportive and productive collaboration reveals yet another way in which motherhood shapes women's rhetoric and rhetorical practices.

Praise, Blame, and the Continuum

I have argued that the god-term Mother and devil-term Woman, gendered rhetorical constructs comprised of well-known qualities and associations, circulate widely within American public discourse. The Mother evokes generally positive connotations, including children, home, love, empathy, protection, nourishment, altruism, morality, religion, self-sacrifice, strength, reproduction, and the nation while the Woman is linked to such negative attributes as self-centeredness, childlessness, work, hysteria, irrationality, the sensual/sexual body, and the public sphere. These god and devil terms afford rhetors shortcuts for praising or blaming women and issues through alignment with either category. What is more, the ground between the two terms also functions rhetorically. Positioning a woman toward the Mother end of the continuum typically elevates her ethical standing; situating a mother toward the Woman end of the continuum usually erodes it. The Woman/Mother continuum (presented in chapter 1) represents persuasive options for promoting or denigrating women and policies through affiliation with or movement toward one of the extremes.

Although the Woman/Mother continuum illuminated the rhetorical operations of motherhood in each of my case studies, it was particularly helpful in decoding pro-life and pro-choice arguments about the UVVA. The bill's proponents, who were predominantly conservative Republicans opposed to abortion, employed a two-person paradigm of pregnancy that permitted them to align their efforts with the god-term Mother. UVVA supporters presented themselves and their legislation as defenders of mothers (and, by extension, their unborn children), in the process establishing bonds with cultural insiders, eliciting emotion, and forging trust. They also suggested, both explicitly and implicitly, that those opposed to their bill were indifferent to codes mandating maternal protection, an accusation that positioned pro-choice advocates toward the Woman end of the continuum and marked them as deviant. Compounding these difficulties, pro-choice rhetors' one-person construct of pregnancy and careful, clinical vocabulary obstructed their access to the rich persuasive resources surrounding motherhood. Their inability to discover an equally compelling alternative undermined the single-victim crime bill.

It is possible, however, to relocate rhetors and issues, moving them from a disadvantageous to a favorable position on the Woman/Mother continuum. As my study of Sanger's ethical rehabilitation indicated, her radical beliefs (for example, privileging female independence over maternal retirement, class strife over social tranquility, women's sexual pleasure over reproductive duty, militant protest over feminine acquiescence) initially aligned her with the devil-term Woman in mainstream press coverage. Her rhetorical embrace of motherhood permitted her to project familiar, reassuring character and to revise public perceptions of birth control, detaching it from socialist, bohemian, immoral associations and recasting it into a respectable issue. In so doing, Sanger repositioned herself and her cause from the Woman to the Mother end of the rhetorical continuum, which ultimately enabled her to attract supporters and expand women's reproductive options. Her persuasive strategy raises an important question: Might the contemporary pro-choice movement benefit from following suit and appropriating motherhood in order to repair damaged ethos, attract new (or estranged) adherents, and protect women's hard-won reproductive freedoms from further erosion?

Contingency and Change

Constructs of sex, gender, and motherhood change in tandem with social, technological, political, medical, and ideological developments. I examined motherhood's ongoing evolution by detailing emergent representations of pregnancy in the controversy over reproductive choice. Over the past sixty years, new imaging technologies have made the contents of women's wombs visible and reshaped public perceptions of gestation and the unborn. Consequently, the organic unity of pregnancy has been displaced by a two-person paradigm that features an expectant woman and an independent fetus, one increasingly portrayed as possessing "needs, interests, and rights separate from and often opposed" to those of its female "host" (Daniels 3). This rhetorical refiguration of motherhood played a pivotal role in congressional debate about the UVVA. Proponents employed various strategies to argue for the fetus's status as a crime victim, exploiting *kairic* opportunities arising from the murder of Laci Peterson and the preborn Conner, depicting the unborn as always/already born children (who, therefore, merited legal protections), and (mis)appropriating images of the deceased to demonstrate fetal personhood. Republican members' construct of pregnancy ensured passage of federal legislation that recognizes the unborn as rights-bearing subjects and creates legal precedent for contesting *Roe v Wade*. Their two-person paradigm, however, would have been impossible without the available visual means generated by new technologies, evidence that the public meaning and persuasive possibilities of the unborn are different now than they were a hundred years ago. The serious consequences that follow from contemporary representations of pregnancy illustrate motherhood's ever-changing signification and never-ending impact on women's civic standing, rights, and interests.

Motherhood—far from being "a single, changeless function," a "limited set of positions," or a "static, 'natural' experience"—is a "moving plurality of potential behaviors always undergoing supervision, revision, and contest, constructed in particularity" (Bowers 18–19). Monitoring its cultural meanings, rhetorical operations, and political implications for women is, therefore, critical. Each of the five themes I examined above—motherhood's emotional resonance, its ethical consequences for women, its shaping of their public involvement and discursive practice, its rhetorical expression in the Woman/Mother continuum, and its constant evolution—offers scholars auspicious territory for further exploration of the topic. One might, for instance, research how motherhood has been understood differently in other historical periods and trace its public manifestations and consequences for women.[2] Another avenue is to decode motherhood's signification and rhetorical deployment in non-Western or indigenous cultures, particularly those with gender systems distinct from the Anglo-American one at the center of my project.[3] Finally, investigating how intersectionality influences the meaning, practice, and regulation of motherhood presents another fruitful locus for scholarship.[4] Motherhood's historical, cultural, and intersectional variations and their effects on women and rhetoric provide exciting opportunities for future study.

Feminist examinations of motherhood in public discourse have the potential to unveil the network of power relations that sustain gender and to disrupt, if only for a moment, the system's self-presentation as universal or divinely ordained. Gendered constructs (like motherhood) issue a "ceaseless, untiring solicitation," an "insidious and inflexible demand," that all subjects recognize themselves in contingent images that are cast as eternal and unchanging (Barthes, *Mythologies* 155–56). Motherhood may appear to be timeless, but it actually bears a date; instead of emanating from nature, it is the product of specific cultural and historical contexts. My feminist analysis in this book resists the monolith of American motherhood and seeks to uncover its artifice. Identifying its origins, development, rhetorical incarnations, and political ramifications and its political implications for women exposes the construct's seams and structuration and creates opportunities for transforming motherhood and gender. After all, power and contention go hand in hand, according to Foucault: Points of resistance are dispersed "over time and space at varying densities" across the social fabric, occasionally resulting in "great radical ruptures" but more often producing fissures that "shift about, fracturing unities and effecting regroupings, furrowing across individuals themselves, cutting them up and remolding them, marking off irreducible regions in them, in their bodies and minds" ("Truth and Power" 96). I bring *Rhetorics of Motherhood* to a close, confident it will attract others to the topic and that our collective efforts will act as Foucauldian points of resistance, heightening awareness of the construction, circulation, and impact of motherhood and thereby contesting dominant systems of gender, knowledge, and power.

Appendix
Notes
Works Cited
Index

Appendix:
"A Message from Diane Nash Bevel to Individuals and Organizations Working for Civil Rights" (30 April 1962)

Note: Nash incorporated her press release into this document, positioning it in paragraphs three and four.

I am surrendering today in Hinds County Court, Jackson, Miss., to serve the sentence imposed on me on a charge of contributing to the delinquency of minors. This charge was filed last summer after I conducted workshops on the philosophy of nonviolence among Jackson youths, preparing them to go on Freedom Rides.

I have issued a brief statement to the press in which I attempt to explain my basic reason for taking this step. This statement says:

"I have decided to surrender myself, abandon further appeal, and serve my sentence of two years, plus as much additional time as it will take to work out my $2000 fine. To appeal further would necessitate my sitting through another trial in a Mississippi court, and I have reached the conclusion that I can no longer cooperate with the evil and unjust court system of this state. I subscribe to the philosophy of nonviolence; this is one of the basic tenets of non-violence—that you refuse to cooperate with evil. The only condition under which I will leave jail will be if the unjust and untrue charges against me are completely dropped."

"Some people have asked me how I can do this when I am expecting my first child in September. I have searched my soul about this and considered it in prayer. I have reached the conclusion that in the long run this will be the best thing I can do for my child. This will be a black child born in Mississippi and thus wherever he is born he will be in prison. I believe that if I go to jail now it may help hasten that day when my child and all children will be free—not only on the day of their birth but for all of their lives."

Records of the Southern Christian Leadership Conference, 1954–1970. Pt. 1. Ed. Randolph Boehm and Blair Hydrick. Bethesda: University Publications of America, 1995. Part 3, Reel 4, Box 126 (0769), 123:43. 1–3.

This is what I said to the press. To you who also are working in this effort for integration, I would like to say more.

I believe the time has come, and is indeed long past, when each of us must make up his mind, when arrested on unjust charges, to serve his sentence and stop posting bonds. I believe that unless we do this our movement loses its power and will never succeed.

We in the nonviolent movement have been talking about jail without bail for two years or more. It is time for us to mean what we say.

We sit in, demonstrate and get beaten up. Yet when we are arrested we immediately post bond and put the matter entirely into the hands of the courts even though we know we won't get justice in these courts.

This is first of all immoral, because the Southern courts in which we are being tried are completely corrupt. We say this is a moral battle, but then we surrender the fight into the legal hands of corrupt courts.

The immorality of these courts involves several factors. They are completely lacking in integrity because we are being arrested and tried on charges that have nothing to do with the real issue. The real reason we are arrested is that we are opposing segregation, but the courts are not honest enough to state this frankly and charge us with this. Instead they hide behind phony charges—breach of peace in Jackson, criminal anarchy in Baton Rouge, conspiracy to violate trespass laws in Talladega, Ala., and so on. We could cite many other examples in many places. Furthermore, in most places we are forced to go on trial in a courtroom that is completely segregated and in a courthouse where all the facilities—drinking fountains, rest rooms, everything—are segregated. Thus the hours that we give to the state for these trials are hours of humiliation and oppression, hours that defile our worth as persons. And then we are asked to pay the bill for this humiliation in court costs. In addition, in many places, the courts are completely corrupt in that they refuse to admit Negroes to the juries.

But over and above the immorality of cooperating with this evil court system, there is an even larger reason why we must begin to stay in jail. If we do not do so, we lose our opportunity to reach the community and society with a great moral appeal and thus bring about basic changes in people and in society.

Our movement is not basically an effort to defeat our opposition. Rather, it is an effort to convert the opposition and redeem society. We should not be trying to win cases; we should be trying to win human beings to a new vision and a new life.

When we leave the jails under bond we lose our opportunity to witness—to prick the conscience of the oppressing group and to appeal to the imagination of the oppressed group and inspire them. We stifle any effort to use what we in the nonviolent movement see as truth force and soul force. We renounce the concept of redemption through suffering. Gandhi said the difference between people who are recklessly breaking the law and those who are standing on a moral principle is that those who stand on principle are willing to take the consequences of their action. When they do this a whole community, indeed a whole nation and the world, may be awakened, and the sights of all society are raised to a new level.

In addition to these basic considerations, there is the very practical matter of skyrocketing expense of continued and numerous legal actions. Our Deep South states have become very smart about this; they are setting bonds high. It simply becomes a physical impossibility for the civil rights movement in America to raise such bonds for great numbers of people. It becomes impossible to raise the money for legal fees and court costs if there are mass arrests and everyone wants to make bond and appeal.

Money can be raised for some test cases. But if we all want to get out on bond, we automatically remove the possibility of a mass movement. There will simply not be enough money to get hundreds of people out on bond in scores of communities and pay the expenses of appealing their cases. And even if there is such money available, there are much better uses to which it can be put in the integration movement.

Let's be realistic. Either we can fight a legal battle with one or two test cases—and in effect abandon our struggle for the several years it takes to litigate the cases in the courts. Or we can resolve to stay in jail and have a movement involving massive numbers.

Some of the considerations I have mentioned are matters of pure principle; they involve the center of what nonviolence means. Some of them are practical considerations, matters of tactics in our struggle. But it is difficult to draw the line between what is principle and what is tactics, because the two merge together. In the long run, right principles are always right tactics.

I think we all realize what it would mean if we had hundreds and thousands of people across the South prepared to go to jail and stay. There can be no doubt that our battle would be won. But we have perhaps erred, each of us, as we have sat and waited for the hundreds to act. History also shows—both recent history and down through the ages—that a few people, even one person, can move mountains. And even if we cannot honestly foresee great effects from our stand, it is my belief that each of us must act on our own conscience—do the thing we know in our hearts is right. In following nonviolence, we have been experimenting with a new and revolutionary method that can bring about a redeemed society. But we have faltered and hesitated—and made many mistakes—because it is new and we are feeling our way. Now I think each of us—regardless of what others may do—must make our own decision, alone and for ourselves. I have made mine.

Notes

1. Theorizing Motherhood in Public Discourse

1. The candidate's ethos and opposition to abortion were further reinforced by daughter Bristol, at the time a pregnant and unmarried high-school junior who would follow in her mother's footsteps and give birth in a difficult situation. Palin's onstage interactions with Trig and Bristol, therefore, provided conservatives with good reasons for supporting her candidacy and convinced many voters of her moral fiber and fitness for office.

2. Although my opening example focuses on Palin, men also employ maternal means of persuasion, as was apparent in the Supreme Court's 2007 ruling on the Partial-Birth Abortion Ban Act, a controversial law that prohibited the late-term abortion procedure known as intact dilation and evacuation (intact D&E). Defenders of the ban argued the procedure was "gruesome," "inhumane," and unnecessary while critics countered that it was medically mandated in certain cases in order to safeguard pregnant women's lives ("Supreme Court Hears Abortion Arguments," n.p.) After six federal courts supported the latter position and struck down the law, an appeal—*Gonzales v. Carhart*—reached the Supreme Court. The High Court overturned the previous federal rulings by a 5–4 majority (that included John Roberts, Samuel Alito, Clarence Thomas, Anthony Kennedy, and Thomas Scalia), upholding the Partial-Birth Abortion Ban Act and handing antiabortion forces "a major victory" ("Supreme Court OKs Abortion Procedure Ban," n.p.).

The majority opinion, drafted by Chief Justice Roberts, displayed evidence of appeals rooted in the motherhood topos. For instance, Roberts presumed that a loving mother/child relationship began at the moment of conception, and he praised the Ban Act for protecting that relationship by obstructing a woman's "choice to abort the infant life" she had "created and sustained":

> It is self-evident that a mother who comes to regret her choice
> to abort must struggle with grief more anguished and sorrow more
> profound when she learns, only after the event, what she once did not
> know: that she allowed a doctor to pierce the skull and vacuum the
> fast-developing brain of her unborn child, a child assuming the human
> form. (*Gonzales v. Carhart* IV: A, legal citations omitted)

The chief justice identified the pregnant woman as a *mother* and the fetus as an *infant life, unborn child,* and *child assuming the human form,* lexical choices that equated the unborn with born children and suggested rights to equal protection under the law. He also depicted the Ban Act as a necessary safeguard, protecting *unborn children* from ill-informed pregnant women and *mothers* from themselves.

The *Gonzales v. Carhart* decision, then, reveals five male justices appropriating discourses about motherhood in order to defend a law that limits pregnant women's medical options and potentially puts them at risk. The impact of the Court's opinion indicates why it is imperative to investigate rhetorics of motherhood and their capacity either to circumscribe or shore up women's reproductive rights, a topic I explore more fully in chapter 4.

3. Weaver argued the importance of grounding ultimate terms in clearly defined, eternal truths; otherwise, god and devil terms might too easily lead the unwary "down the roads of hatred and bigotry" (232). I, too, believe in the persuasive capacity of language that "sound[s] like the very gospel of one's society" but modify Weaver's rhetorical theory by positing god and devil terms as socially contingent and, therefore, mutable, a postmodern interpretation that would undoubtedly elicit protest from him. With that modification in place, I find the integration of god and devil terms with cultural scripts, values, and codes a powerful lever for unpacking the construction of gender difference and motherhood.

4. Kimberlé Crenshaw's observations regarding the construction of difference also help to unravel the hierarchical relations between the Woman and Mother outlined here. Power, she argues, clusters around identity categories (such as gender, race, class, sexual orientation, and so on), privileging some groups while subordinating others. Although power is "exercised simply through the process of categorization," its real impact circulates in the values associated with particular categories, values that foster hierarchy and shape social and material conditions (1296–97). Echelons operate, I argue, not only across but also within gender categories (in other words, between men and women and also among women); further, they provide rhetors with contrasting categories —such as Woman and Mother—that are useful for praising or blaming women. As Crenshaw notes, uncovering categorical constructions and their maintenance over time constitutes an important critical project, one capable of unveiling "processes of subordination and the various ways those processes are experienced by people who are subordinated and people who are privileged by them" (1297). Understanding the rhetorical construction and impact of the Mother and Woman, therefore, has the potential to reveal how gender subordination is sustained through the processes of categorization, evaluation, and hierarchy described above.

5. Widespread negative perceptions of Liuzzo's character were reflected, for instance, in the comments of Selma sheriff Jim Clark, who remarked, "I have five children too. But the night [Liuzzo's murder] happened my wife was at home with the children where she belongs" (qtd. in Stanton 54). Similarly, the

Ladies Home Journal (July 1965) published survey responses to the query, "Do you think that Mrs. Viola Liuzzo, the Detroit civil rights worker who was killed in the Alabama shooting incident, had a right to leave her five children to risk her life for a social cause or not?" More than half answered that she should have stayed home, with one respondent stating, "I don't feel that I have the right to endanger myself and to leave my children motherless. The sorrow they would feel at the loss of a mother is greater than any cause" (qtd. in Stanton 170–71). These remarks reveal that mothering was still strongly associated with the private sphere in the mid-1960s and the severe penalties that befell mothers who departed from their assigned realm.

6. Within disciplines other than rhetoric, motherhood has received substantial attention and produced an enormous body of work. The following feminist scholarship, written from other disciplinary perspectives, has been particularly important to my project: Paula Gunn Allen, *The Sacred Hoop: Recovering the Feminine in American Indian Traditions*; Donna Bassin, Margaret Honey, and Meryle Kaplan, eds., *Representations of Motherhood*; Toni Bowers, *The Politics of Motherhood: British Writing and Culture, 1680–1760*; Patricia Hill Collins, *Black Feminist Thought: Knowledge, Consciousness, and the Politics of Empowerment*; Patrice DiQuinzio, *The Impossibility of Motherhood: Feminism, Individualism, and the Problem of Mothering*; Evelyn Nakano Glenn, Grace Change, and Linda Forcey, eds., *Mothering: Ideology, Experience, and Agency*; Sarah Hardy and Caroline Wiedmer, eds., *Motherhood and Space: Configurations of the Maternal through Politics, Home, and the Body*; E. Ann Kaplan, *Motherhood and Representation: The Mother in Popular Culture and Melodrama*; Amber Kinser, *Motherhood and Feminism*; Julie Kipp, *Romanticism, Maternity, and the Body Politic*; Rebecca Kukla, *Mass Hysteria: Medicine, Culture, and Mother's Bodies*; Sharon Meagher and Patrice DiQuinzio, eds., *Women and Children First: Feminism, Rhetoric, and Public Policy*; Andrea O'Reilly, *Mother Outlaws: Theories and Practices of Empowered Motherhood*; Adrienne Rich, *Of Woman Born: Motherhood as Experience and Institution*; Sara Ruddick, *Maternal Thinking: Toward a Politics of Peace*; Ann Snitow, "Feminism and Motherhood: An American Reading." Additionally, two resources affiliated with the Motherhood Initiative for Research and Community Involvement (formerly the Association for Research on Mothering) have been helpful sources of multidisciplinary academic and activist analyses of the subject—the *Journal of the Motherhood Initiative* (formerly the *Journal of the Association for Research on Mothering*) and Demeter Press.

7. This project builds upon the recovery efforts of a great many feminist historiographers, too many, in fact, to acknowledge fully here. A sampling of that work includes Karlyn Kohrs Campbell's *Man Cannot Speak for Her: A Critical Study of Early Feminist Rhetoric;* Vicki Collins's "The Speaker Respoken: Rhetoric as Feminist Methodology;" Jane Donawerth's *Conversational Rhetoric: The Rise and Fall of a Women's Tradition, 1600–1900*; Jessica Enoch's

Refiguring Rhetorical Education: Women Teaching African American, Native American, and Chicano/a Students, 1865–1911; Cheryl Glenn's *Rhetoric Retold: Regendering the Tradition from Antiquity through the Renaissance*; Shirley Wilson Logan's *"We Are Coming": The Persuasive Discourse of Nineteenth-Century Black Women*; Carol Mattingly's *Well-Tempered Women: Nineteenth-Century Temperance Rhetoric* and *Appropriate[ing] Dress: Women's Rhetorical Style in Nineteenth-Century America*; Roxanne Mountford's *The Gendered Pulpit: Preaching in American Protestant Spaces*; Jacqueline Jones Royster's *Traces of a Stream: Literacy and Social Change among African-American Women*; Wendy Sharer's *Voice and Vote: Women's Organizations and Public Literacy, 1915–1930*, as well as edited collections by Catherine Hobbs, Andrea Lunsford, Molly Wertheimer, Christine Sutherland and Rebecca Sutcliffe, and Hildy Miller and Lillian Bridwell-Bowles. Feminist retheorizations of rhetoric also inform my analysis and include Cheryl Glenn's *Unspoken: The Rhetoric of Silence* and Krista Ratcliffe's *Anglo-American Feminist Challenges to the Rhetorical Traditions: Virginia Woolf, Mary Daly, Adrienne Rich* and *Rhetorical Listening: Identification, Gender, Whiteness*. For a comprehensive overview of the field of feminist rhetorics—including its genesis and development, its guiding research strands and concerns, and its major publication and presentation venues—see the introduction to Lindal Buchanan and Kathleen Ryan's *Walking and Talking Feminist Rhetorics: Landmark Essays and Controversies*.

8. A note on terminology: To minimize confusion, I employ the adjective *maternal* to denote persuasive means derived from the motherhood topos—i.e., *maternal* rhetorics—and to distinguish them from *maternalist* discourse or *maternalism*, a rhetorical strategy developed by nineteenth-century women. A number of scholars have examined the advisability of employing motherhood rhetorically to justify women's public participation and promote their political objectives. For arguments focusing on its disadvantages for women, see Karen Foss and Kathy Domenici's "Haunting Argentina: Synecdoche in the Protests of the Mothers of the Plaza de Mayo"; Lynn Stearney's "Feminism, Ecofeminism, and the Maternal Archetype: Motherhood as a Feminine Universal"; and Joan Tronto's *Moral Boundaries: A Political Argument for an Ethic of Care*. For more favorable assessments of motherhood in public discourse, see Bonnie J. Dow and Mari Boor Tonn's "'Feminine Style' and Political Judgment in the Rhetoric of Ann Richards"; Valeria Fabj's "Motherhood as Political Voice: The Rhetoric of the Mothers of Plaza de Mayo"; Seth Koven and Sonya Michel's *Mothers of a New World: Maternalist Politics and the Origins of Welfare States*; Gisela Norat's "Women Staging Coups through Mothering"; Sara Ruddick's *Maternal Thinking: Toward a Politics of Peace*; Amy Swerdlow's *Women Strike for Peace: Traditional Motherhood and Radical Politics in the 1960s*; and Mari Boor Tonn's "Militant Motherhood: Labor's Mary Harris 'Mother' Jones."

9. Laqueur's account of the one-sex model has been criticized for oversimplifying "ancient medical and philosophical views about sexual difference" (Aune

337) and for slighting prescientific systems that "*did* elaborate differences of kind between two sexes" (Altman and Nightenhelser, n.p.; Park and Nye 56). His assertion that the two-sex model gained widespread acceptance by the end of the nineteenth century has also been questioned, with scholar Susan Ullman, for instance, countering that the process is still underway in medical and scientific circles where "male" continues to function as the prototype (117). Finally, Laqueur's assumptions regarding the prevalence of a heterosexual matrix have also come under fire. However, despite shortcomings and critiques, his central thesis regarding shifting sexual paradigms continues to be broadly accepted and used within the field of gender studies.

10. Rousseau's convictions regarding childrearing's civic consequences attracted medical, political, and social attention to motherhood as well, as was evident, for instance, in eighteenth-century controversies over breastfeeding. The philosopher's belief in the importance of sustained, intimate contact between mother and child led him to decry the popular practice of wet-nursing. Typically, infants were sent off to the country to be nursed and raised by others during the first year of life, an arrangement that encouraged social chaos, according to Rousseau. The remedy to civic dissolution and depravity lay in mothers' milk: "Let mothers deign to nurse their children, [and] morals will reform themselves, nature's sentiments will be awakened in every heart, the state will be repopulated" (46). New perceptions of mothers' influence on social order encouraged increased surveillance of the maternal body. Heightened medical interest was reflected in William Cadogan's influential *Essay upon Nursing and the Management of Children from Birth to Three Years of Age* (1748), which advocated male experts' supervision of breastfeeding: The "Method of Nursing has too long been fatally left to the Management of Women, who cannot be supposed to have proper knowledge to fit them for such a task, notwithstanding, they look upon it as their own Province" (3). He called, instead, for those with "Philosophic Knowledge of Nature, to be acquir'd only by learned Observation and Experience"—i.e., male physicians—to replace women as authorities on the subject. Legislators, likewise, gave nursing due consideration. Rebecca Kukla observes that in pre-Revolutionary France, less than 5 percent of Parisian infants were breastfeed by their mothers (52). In 1793, however, the National Convention mandated maternal breastfeeding and offered financial support to nursing mothers (so that "military and generous virtues could flow, with maternal milk, into the hearts of all the nurslings of France"); within a decade, more than 50 percent of the city's women breastfed their own children (52–53). As the above examples suggest, a confluence of philosophical, medical, and political attention over the course of the eighteenth century constructed motherhood as civically significant, institutionalized it in ways that promoted new maternal practices, and contributed to its cultural reformation.

11. Many feminist scholars have observed that "separate spheres" were more rhetorical device than reality during the nineteenth century (see, for instance,

Linda Kerber's "Separate Spheres"). Motherhood, nevertheless, became firmly connected to the private sphere during that period, an association that continues to inform its cultural coding and rhetorical function to this day.

12. My allusions to the experience and institution of motherhood are drawn, of course, from Adrienne Rich's landmark feminist analysis *Of Woman Born*. She makes a critical distinction between the experience ("the *potential relationship* of any woman to her powers of reproduction and to children") and the institution of motherhood ("which aims at ensuring that that potential—and all women—shall remain under male control") (13). Grounded in the body, the experience of motherhood encompasses the complex physical sensations and profound positive, negative, and conflicted emotions that accompany pregnancy, delivery, nursing, adoption, and child rearing. Rich movingly details how anger, frustration, and sometimes even violence are as inherent to maternal experience as love and tenderness. Her honesty freed women to discuss motherhood candidly and to contest its frequently idyllic and unrealistic cultural depiction. Rich's *Of Woman Born has* inspired an avalanche of scholarship on motherhood and demonstrates women's ability to "talk back" to cultural codes and institutions and (slowly) revise oppressive systems.

13. During the antebellum period, motherhood sometimes halted the most promising oratorical careers as was the case with Frances Wright and Angelina Grimké Weld (Buchanan, *Regendering* 121–23). However, it more often interrupted women's rhetorical commitments for a time, with some mothers returning to public speaking a few months after their children's births and others waiting for decades. Although the length of interruptions varied, the interludes themselves influenced the arc of women's rhetorical careers. Because of multiple or sustained periods devoted to bearing and raising children, women who were both mothers and rhetors were often older when they returned to (or even began) their public speaking careers, and they frequently remained active in those careers far longer than their male counterparts, working well into their seventies, eighties, or nineties. Sadly, motherhood's capacity to constrain women's rhetorical careers is not restricted to the nineteenth century but continues to this day.

2. From "Wild Woman Writer" to "Mother of Two": Margaret Sanger, Birth Control, and Ethos Repair

1. In naming her column "What Every Girl Ought to Know," Sanger joined ranks with late-nineteenth-century female reformers and physicians who wrote candidly about sex. As Carolyn Skinner details in "'The Purity of Truth': Nineteenth-Century American Women Physicians Write about Delicate Topics," other popular publications sported similar titles, including Mary Wood-Allen's *What a Young Woman Ought to Know* (1892) and *What a Young Girl Ought to Know* (1897) as well as Emma Drake's *What a Young Wife Ought to Know* (1901). Sanger's nursing background, education, and experience qualified her

to contribute to the burgeoning sex-education genre, and the intertextuality of her column's title connected it to an established series of work, making its focus immediately identifiable and granting authority to the novice writer.

At this early point in her career, Sanger advanced the "classical liberal argument" that possession and regulation of one's own body was the bedrock of political autonomy and "individual freedom, delimiting the domain of government authority" (McCann 31). On that basis, women had the right to determine when or whether to have children through the use of contraception and/or abortion. She also embraced the new psychology, which posited that men's and women's sex drives were equally strong and that "sexual love was healthy, natural for women" (34), a view antithetical to nineteenth-century assumptions regarding "good" women's disinterest in procreation. Sanger's radical stance on women's sexuality and bodily self-possession stirred "cultural anxiety over the heterosexually independent woman" and alienated many moderate and conservative readers (43).

2. Sanger was already firmly committed to challenging and changing the Comstock laws. Facing dire consequences for discussing birth control in general terms within the *Woman Rebel,* she decided to push further and provide specific instructions on its practice. To that end, she drafted the pamphlet *Family Limitation,* and its simple language and straightforward illustrations detailed a variety of contraceptive methods and devices, including *coitus interruptus,* douches, sponges, condoms, and diaphragms (or pessaries). Once Sanger left the United States and was safely on route to England and exile, she directed supporters to distribute 100,000 copies of the pamphlet (Katz 91; Sanger, *Margaret* 112–17).

3. The construct of separate spheres is useful for delineating in broad strokes gender ideals and divisions that emerged in the early republic; however, as numerous feminist historians have noted—including Ellen DuBois ("Politics"), Linda Kerber ("Separate Spheres"), and Joan W. Scott—the public/private binary oversimplifies what were, in fact, varied and changing arrangements of labor, practice, and space.

4. *Birth Control,* thus, contains vestiges of the militant, anticapitalist perspective typical of Sanger's discourse prior to exile. To illustrate, a cadre of uninformed and grasping socialites become aware of Sanger's plans to bring contraceptives to the poor and protest that both "public morals" and "sacred institutions are menaced" (*Papers on Appeal* 80). One wealthy participant asks his peers, "Why, if the lower classes do not continue to have children who will act as your servants—who will perform the labor in the industries over which you of the Superior Class rule?" (81). The specter of a labor shortage is frightening enough to send the collection basket circling the room and sets the stage for Sanger's eventual imprisonment.

5. Surprisingly, birth control and eugenics were popular subjects for films and plays in 1917. The silent pictures *Race Suicide* and *Birth* (the latter produced by the Eugenic Film Company) were both in release, and their showings were

frequently restricted to women only and preceded by short talks on childbirth and mothering (*Hudson [NY] Republican*, 19 March 1917; *New York American*, 1 April 1917). Meanwhile, Howard McKent Barnes's drama *Her Unborn Child* also opened in 1917. Although it took a negative position on contraception, the play, nevertheless, contributed to "the birth-control discussion which rages all about" (*[Philadelphia] North American*, 13 March 1917). Four touring companies took the play around the country; however, as the social and political climate grew increasingly conservative, citizens protested, and officials reviewed the play, with some cities banning its production altogether ("Salem Bars Play on Birth Control," *Boston American*, 7 May 1917). (Except where noted otherwise, all newspaper accounts cited in this note are in Sanger, File no. 6.)

Sanger's fight for birth control generated her own film, of course, but it inspired others too. Lois Weber's *Where Are My Children?* (1916), for instance, was reviewed as "an excellent propaganda for disseminating knowledge on birth control," a topic that "since the Margaret Sanger case . . . [had] been discussed in the daily prints" and was, therefore, being "presented in the motions pictures as well" (*Boston American*, 2 July 1916, in Sanger, File no. 5). Weber's film was so popular that it produced a sequel, *The Hand that Rocks the Cradle* (1917), which had the misfortune of being released around the time of Sanger's own picture. *Birth Control* was scheduled for a 6 May 1917 premiere, and newspaper accounts suggest strong interest in the production, noting the presence of "thousands of people" on opening night (*New York Call*, 7 May 1917). Commissioner Bell, however, effectively banned the film by threatening to revoke the licenses of playhouses that showed it, and a week later, he proceeded to do the same with *Hand That Rocks the Cradle* (*New York Tribune*, 7 May 1917 and 14 May 1917). Although the producers of both films sought injunctions overturning Bell's decision, the Appellate Division ultimately upheld his rulings, adding its own "disapproval of birth control films" (*New York Dramatic Mirror*, 21 July 1917, in Sanger, File no. 5). Despite the films' closings, the controversies that surrounded them, nevertheless, helped Sanger's cause by interjecting arguments for and against contraception into the public arena.

6. I am not suggesting that Sanger's embrace of maternal ethos was solely strategic or constituted a false front. By all accounts, she blamed herself for her daughter's death, convinced she could have prevented the child's final illness had she not left the country. Although she grieved Peggy's loss the rest of her life, the rhetor, nevertheless, employed it to promote herself and birth control. One can trace the transformation of private maternal anguish into a form suitable for public consumption through the journal entries Sanger composed during her 1914 journey into exile. They convey distress at separation from her children, and some address her young daughter directly: "Dear Peggy how my love goes out to you—I could weep from loneliness for you—just to touch your soft chubby hands—but work is to be done dear—work to help to make your path easier—& those who come after you" (qtd. in Katz 98). Sanger later incorporated

the sentiment into her 1938 autobiography, using the maternal longing produced by her flight from America to explain her next violation of the Comstock laws: "My soul was sick and my heart empty for those I loved; the one gleam in this dreadful night of despair was the faint hope that my effort [distributing the pamphlet *Family Limitation*] might, perhaps, make Peggy's future easier" (*Margaret* 122). The account implied that only a true mother could absent herself from a beloved daughter in order to make the world a better place for her, an enthymeme suggesting that motherhood was integral to Sanger's ethos by 1938.

7. The acumen of the Committee of 100 was evident soon after its formation. On 22 Jan 1917, Byrne was sentenced to thirty days in Blackwell's Island Penitentiary and, in protest, quickly embarked on a hunger strike. Her refusal to eat or drink attracted a great deal of media attention, especially once her health began to deteriorate, and spurred the Committee into action: On 27 January, it sent a delegation to lobby influential Congressmen in Washington, D.C.; on 29 January, it sponsored a huge rally at Carnegie Hall to publicize Byrne's condition, an event that drew an estimated 3,000 people and raised $1,000 for Sanger, Byrne, and Mindell's legal defense (Chesler 154); and on 3 February, it procured a pardon from New York Governor Charles Whitman and began making arrangements for Byrne's early release (Lade 123). As these efforts suggest, the financial resources and social connections of elite women contributed enormously to the cause. Sanger's son Grant recalled, "You thought they didn't have a brain in their head or an interest in anything at all, [but then] these women would gather themselves up with their furs and their chauffeurs and they'd go down and see the mayor of the city of New York. He'd have to see them because they were in such a position in town" (qtd. in Franks 39). Access to and influence on the powerful played a pivotal role in moving birth control away from the margins and into the mainstream.

3. Motherhood, Civil Rights, and Remembrance: Recuperating Diane Nash

1. According to the *Jackson Advocate*, Nash was charged with four counts of contributing to the delinquency of minors as a result of conducting workshops on nonviolent resistance for Jackson youth. She was tried and sentenced to serve two years and pay a $2000 fine by the City Court; the case was later appealed to the County Court and she was free on bond while awaiting retrial ("Dianne Nash" 1, 6).

2. Nash comported herself as an exemplar in hopes of changing civil-right protestors' expectations and attitudes, inspiring courageous action, and revising movement policy, and the success of her rhetorical performance was apparent that day, Her refusal to leave the white-only section of the courtroom prompted Luvaghn Brown and Jesse Harris, leaders of the Jackson Nonviolent Movement, to follow suit, so all three went to jail on contempt charges ("Miss. Judge" 56).

3. Nash has stated that her pregnancy created a bad public-relations situation for Mississippi authorities ("Interview" 2008). Although Moore sent her

to jail briefly for openly defying segregation in his courtroom, she believes he felt compelled to do something immediately in order to reassert authority. In the long term, he was simply not willing to deal with the negative publicity that would have followed from sending a well-known, pregnant civil-rights figure to prison for two years. Pressure and attention are focused on the system when protesters are incarcerated, she explained; keeping her out of jail removed both.

4. John Gage defines the enthymeme as "any statement made in reasoned discourse that is accompanied by substantiation in the form of one or more premises" likely to be familiar to the audience (223). A rhetor rarely details an enthymeme's complete line of reasoning (in the form of major premise, minor premise, and conclusion) and, instead, omits material that she can safely predict is known by readers. According to Aristotle, their contribution of a missing premise or conclusion is crucial, for it "connects the assumed beliefs of the audience with the conclusion of the rhetor by means of invented arguments" (223). The real marker of an enthymeme, then, is not that it has a missing premise or conclusion but that unstated material draws upon communal beliefs inculcated through shared cultural scripts and codes.

5. For other examples of the giant fighter narrative, see Rosetta Ross's *Witnessing and Testifying: Black Women, Religion, and Civil Rights* and Nash's entry in *The King Encyclopedia*.

6. Bevel and Lafayette faced five charges for "corrupting minors," each carrying a potential fine of $2,000 and two-year jail term (Halberstam 394). The men spent two weeks in jail but were released when NAACP lawyer Jack Young plea bargained a suspended sentence for them, with the proviso that they leave Jackson. Bevel and Lafayette rejected the conditions, fired Young, and represented themselves in court. Bevel declared that he was not corrupting black children in Mississippi; the true culprit was the state of Mississippi, with its "system of segregation which denied them their basic rights as well as decent schools and decent jobs, and their innate dignity as American citizens" (Halberstam 395). Although the judge sentenced Bevel and Lafayette to the maximum jail time and fines, he suspended their sentences, warning them to expect no mercy if they appeared in his court again.

7. Robnett's purpose is to demonstrate women's leadership role in the civil-rights movement, and it sometimes leads her to gloss over complicating factors. She does not mention, for instance, that Nash posted bond and left jail after her initial sentencing (fall 1961) or that her decision to suspend her appeal and serve her term occurred months later (spring 1962). Telescoping events in this manner enables Robnett to tell her tale concisely, to present her protagonist as decisive from the start, and to focus on Nash's rhetoric and efforts to promote jail-no-bail policy rather than on the events leading up to them.

8. One might even argue that King's appreciation for jail-no-bail policy profoundly shaped his future actions, culminating in his arrest and imprisonment

during the 1963 Birmingham campaign and production of the acclaimed "Letter from Birmingham Jail."

4. Changing Constructs of Motherhood: Pregnancy and Personhood in Laci and Conner's Law

1. Late twentieth-century developments in medical technology have made the unborn more accessible, visible, public, and, hence, rhetorical than ever before. Such medical tools and procedures as X-rays, sonographs, ultrasounds, and fetal surgery effectively made the female peritoneum transparent, its contents available for scrutiny (Duden 7). Photography has also played a noteworthy role in revolutionizing visual constructions of pregnancy in public discourse. When Lennart Nilsson's groundbreaking photograph of an eighteen-week-old fetus, floating weightlessly in what appeared to be outer space, appeared on a 1965 cover of *Life* magazine, it was immediately embraced by popular culture and accepted as a realistic depiction of the unborn: "The curled-up profile, with its enlarged head and finlike arms, suspended in its balloon of amniotic fluid, is by now so familiar that not even most feminists question its authenticity" (Petchesky, "Foetal Images" 174–75). Photographs of the solitary fetus suggest that it is "primary and autonomous" by rendering the expectant woman "absent or peripheral," a relatively new but rampant representation of the maternal body that encourages the separation of a woman from her pregnancy (Kukla 110).

2. From the first, the antiabortion movement has been sensitive to the persuasive potential of fetal imagery and has used it to craft forceful visual arguments against *Roe v Wade*. Its careful selection and dissemination of late second- and third-term fetal photographs have erased "the wide variety of beings that constitute developing unborn human life-forms—the blastocyst, embryo, fetus, viable baby" (Condit 82). By emphasizing similarities between the born and unborn, the movement has successfully cast the fetus as a child, thereby creating a vulnerable, sympathetic, and new rhetorical figure (82–85).

Fetal images are highly rhetorical artifacts in terms of their construction, selection, and use in public discourse (see Condit, Petchesky, Gilbert, Kukla, and Duden). They portray the unborn as separate, independent beings through a number of visual strategies, including perspective. Typically, such pictures depict the fetus as "solitary, dangling in the air (or in its sac) with nothing to connect it to any life-support system but a 'clearly defined umbilical cord' . . . Nowhere is there any reference to the pregnant woman" (Petchesky, "Foetal Images" 174–75). Additionally, fetal images distributed by the antiabortion movement generally show the unborn after the age of seven weeks, the point when it begins to assume human appearance (Gilbert, n.p.). To endow the fetus with the looks and characteristics of a living child, photographs either show it sucking a thumb or else focus on its tiny fingers and toes, strategies that, again, blur the boundary between the born and the unborn. Depicting the fetus as a miniature, vulnerable, helpless infant not only invites viewers' care and protection but also elicits strong emotions, effects that antiabortion groups have encouraged in order to forward the claim that personhood begins at conception, rather than at viability or birth.

3. As Jacqueline Jones Royster observes, feminists' minds, bodies, hearts, and souls often "operate collectively" in their scholarship ("Introduction" 7). I take a moment, therefore, to acknowledge my own investment in the issues examined in this chapter. Like most women, I am deeply conflicted about the moral complexities of abortion. Neither the pregnant woman nor the unborn come with "ready-made stable boundaries"; instead, the "maternal body incarnates one human at the beginning of pregnancy and two at the end of it, and it is by no means clear how to tell a coherent story of this passage" (Kukla 3). While aware of the ambiguities inherent to the gestational process, I am, nevertheless, a staunch supporter of women's right to decide whether or not to continue a pregnancy to full term and so am committed to preserving safe, legal abortion in the United States. Protecting choice, however, is only one of many issues at stake within the broad arena of reproductive justice, a more comprehensive analytic that embraces the full range of subjects (including "sexism, poverty, racism, xenophobia, and homophobia") that affect women's fertility, pregnancy, delivery, and pre- and post-natal care (Hayden, "Revitalizing" 122). Therefore, it is not sufficient to protect legal abortion without also addressing the access issues that plague poor and rural women. At present, more than eighty-seven percent of U.S. counties lack an abortion provider, so "the legal right to abortion remains an empty promise for women who lack the financial resources and geographic proximity to actually realize this right" (122). When one extends such analysis beyond national borders, the complexities multiply exponentially, indicating the importance of adopting a holistic, comprehensive approach to women's reproductive health and control.

4. Questions surrounding the beginning of personhood and permissibility of abortion have stimulated discussion since the classical period. An influential pronouncement on the subject by Aristotle and his followers, for example, asserted that animation occurred in the male fetus at forty days and the female at eighty, a timeline that was also maintained by early Christian fathers, including Augustine (*Roe v Wade* 410 U.S. 113 [1973], notes 22, 27). The Catholic Church, however, typically spoke of ensoulment, rather than animation, as the point at which the soul entered the body and life began. That moment was conventionally marked by the pregnant woman's first perception of fetal movement (or quickening). For most of its history, the Catholic Church condoned abortion prior to ensoulment and "reserved excommunication only for those who aborted *after* quickening" (McLaren 109–10), a policy that persisted well into the nineteenth century.

The Church's stance influenced the development of English common law, which also did not regard abortion prior to quickening as an indictable offense. Furthermore, because quickening was felt and announced by women, the identification of life's beginning rested in their hands, granting them considerable authority: "A woman only became officially and publicly pregnant when she felt her fetus . . . move inside her" (Epstein 112). An abortion could, therefore, take place without penalty until a woman announced that quickening had occurred. Although seventeenth-century jurists considered abortion after that point a "misprision" or "non-capital common law offence," evidence in such cases was almost impossible to obtain, so there were virtually no prosecutions and "the law was in effect a dead letter" (McLaren 122).

Legal, medical, and religious views that, for centuries, had moved in tandem began to diverge during the Enlightenment. As male physicians displaced midwives, authority over pregnancy moved from women's into men's hands, and both the womb and its contents inched into the public realm. Maternal bodies became "objects of rigorous scientific surveillance and attention" and were "inserted into the public institutional spaces of professional obstetrics, public benefits programs, anatomy textbooks, family law, and medical education" (Kukla 66). As a result of these changes and the paradigm shift from a one- to a two-sex model (detailed in chapter 1), legal definitions of personhood underwent scrutiny as well. The most noteworthy eighteenth-century expression occurred in William Blackstone's *Commentaries on the Laws of England* (1769), which recognized life as the "immediate gift of God, a right inherent by nature in each individual" and marked its beginning as the first stirring within the womb (qtd. in Curran 61). Blackstone detailed legal consequences for harming the quickened fetus either through abortion or violence and categorized either act as "a heinous misdemeanour." Although he followed tradition in demarcating quickening as the point when society incurred an obligation to safeguard the unborn, Blackstone's attribution of natural rights (in particular, the right to life) to the fetus was a legal milestone.

Over the course of the nineteenth century, the maternal body continued to assume new meanings in legal, medical, and religious circles. In 1803, English law made abortion after quickening a felony offense and, for the first time, also imposed penalties for abortion *prior* to quickening. Most of the legislation, however, was directed toward "purveyors of purported abortifacients" that resulted in women's deaths rather than "the act of abortion *per se*" (McLaren 136). Stated differently, the perceived victim in abortion-related deaths was the pregnant woman, not the fetus. Many scholars, including Angus McLaren, trace the impetus for nineteenth-century revisions of abortion law to doctors' continuing efforts to professionalize and gain control over fertility and pregnancy. Physicians' growing influence was apparent in the demise of quickening as a forensic concept, a nonscientific notion they disliked because it gave "the word of the patient [or woman] . . . as much legal weight as that of the doctor" (139). England's *Offences against the Person Act* (1837), therefore, abolished quickening as a legitimate demarcation and based the law, instead, on the scientific "findings of physiology" (143).

At this time, antiabortion laws crossed the Atlantic and made their appearance in the United States. In 1821, Connecticut was the first state to criminalize abortion following quickening, unleashing a "wave of abortion-control laws" throughout the 1830s and 1840s (Hull and Hoffer 20–21). Although their initial purpose was to safeguard the lives of pregnant women, stringent statutes passed between 1840 and 1880 outlawed the procedure entirely unless needed for therapeutic purposes. In 1869, the Catholic Church followed suit, reversing its traditional tolerance for abortion prior to quickening and condemning it "at any time in a pregnancy. By the end of the century, the Catholic hierarchy . . . concluded that even therapeutic abortions were a sin" (32). The changed religious and legal status of abortion reflected a growing preoccupation with controlling women's reproductive bodies and protecting the unborn, a trend that has not only persisted but intensified (34–35).

5. The *Roe v. Wade* decision recognized a constitutional "right of personal privacy" in certain realms, including "a woman's decision whether or not to terminate her pregnancy" (410 U.S. 113 [1973], VIII, 18). Feminist scholars have vigorously critiqued *Roe*'s grounding in privacy rights because it leaves lawmakers the option of redefining personhood (say, by moving its origination point prior to birth) and thereby jeopardizing the decision. In *Abortion and Woman's Choice: The State, Sexuality, and Reproductive Freedom*, for instance, Rosalind Petchesky argues that recognizing women as a class meriting equal protection under the law (their rights, in that case, deriving from the equal protection clauses in the Fifth and Fourteenth Amendments) would have proved a sounder basis for the decision. Julia Epstein, meanwhile, holds that the doctrine of bodily integrity—which includes "the rights to be left alone, to refuse medical treatment, and to have possession of and power over one's own person"—offers a surer foundation for reproductive choice (125).

The rationale of the *Roe* decision has been repeatedly challenged over the years. The Supreme Court has permitted states to restrict abortion funding as well as women's access to abortion services, claiming these actions have no impact upon the right to privacy. Additionally, it has extended the period of the state's protective interest in/obligation to the unborn. In *Planned Parenthood v. Casey* (1992), the Court replaced *Roe*'s original trimester framework with a new standard of "undue burden," holding that "the state has a profound interest in protecting fetal life throughout pregnancy, not just at the point of viability. The state can therefore enact obstacles to abortion as long as they are not so substantial as to be unduly burdensome" (Roth 21). In practice, women's ability to procure abortions has been severely eroded because privacy (rather than class protection or bodily integrity) served as the foundation for *Roe*, resulting in a deeply flawed and extremely vulnerable decision.

6. Serrin Foster, former president of Feminists for Life of America, highlighted troubling loopholes in federal crime statutes during congressional

committee hearings on the UVVA. She related the "tragic story of a pregnant woman killed in the 1995 Oklahoma City bombing":

> After years of trying to have a child, Carrie and Michael Lenz, Jr., were overjoyed to learn that she was carrying their son, whom they named Michael Lenz III. Carrying a copy of the sonogram, Carrie went to work early the next morning to show coworkers the first photo of baby Michael. She and Michael were killed, along with three other pregnant women and their unborn children, when the Alfred P. Murrah Federal Building exploded on April 19, 1995. This father's agony was multiplied later when he saw that the memorial named only his wife, not his son, as a victim. In the eyes of the federal government, there was no second victim. Timothy McVeigh was never held accountable for killing Michael Lenz's namesake. (qtd. in Marzilli 73)

In this case, failure to acknowledge the additional loss of a pregnancy added to Mr. Lenz's anguish and suggests why the issue of fetal personhood matters so much to survivors of violent crime.

7. Many congressional members who initially opposed the two-victim crime bill voted for it following defeat of the single-victim bill. In the Senate, for example, the MPA failed narrowly by a vote of 50 to 49 (Senate S3151). Although Feinstein reminded colleagues that the UVVA's definition of the *unborn child* would create federal precedent capable of abrogating women's reproductive rights, the bill passed the Senate by a wide margin, 61 to 38 (Senate S3167). The political peril of not supporting *mothers* and *preborn children* likely accounts for the eleven members who ultimately changed allegiance and voted for the two-victim crime bill.

Conclusion: Interrogating Motherhood, Transforming Gender

1. Depending upon the rhetorical situation, feminist objectives may either be explicit or implicit. Given a generally negative climate in the United States today, some progressive groups are employing the mantle of motherhood to obscure feminist goals of protecting or advancing women's status. This is the strategy adopted by the grassroots organization MomsRising.org, for example. Founded in 2006 by Joan Blades and Kristin Rowe-Finkbeiner, it is currently the largest organization in the burgeoning mothers' movement in North America. Moms-Rising.org has, in a few short years, produced a book and DVD (both entitled *The Motherhood Manifesto*) and a robust website, detailing the problematic position of American women—who continue to assume primary responsibility for childrearing and caring labor while also sustaining outside employment—and advocating national and state campaigns to change it. Although three-quarters of U.S. mothers are in the labor force, "legislative policies and workplaces" are "stuck in a 1950's mentality" that assumes the presence of a full-time mother in

the home ("Crisis," n.p.). This presumption produces utterly inadequate support systems that, in turn, create a plethora of interrelated economic, medical, educational, and professional obstacles for American women and their children. MomsRising.org's planks for reforming business practices and public policy address these inequities. To promote its vision, the organization mines motherhood rhetorically in order to create exigence, attract a constituency to work for change, and gain concessions from assemblies and corporations that have typically ignored the needs of working mothers. By framing problems and solutions in terms of mothers' rights and responsibilities to children, the organization pursues feminist objectives without using the *F*-word.

2. To suggest possibilities here, I refer readers to my essay "A Study of Maternal Rhetoric: Anne Hutchinson, Monsters, and the Antinomian Controversy." Hutchinson was a leading figure in the religious, economic, and political dispute that fractured the Massachusetts Bay Colony in the late 1630s. Puritans elders, in their efforts to maintain secular and spiritual control, used the rhetor's delivery of malformed child (or a "monster" as such births were called in the seventeenth century) as evidence of heresy, thereby discrediting Hutchinson and silencing her supporters. Such interpretation and rhetorical use of women's offspring points to a different perception of conception and pregnancy. Prior to the Enlightenment, Marie-Hélene Huet explains, many believed that the natural order called for the father's image to be replicated in his children and that malformed progeny, instead, reflected the thoughts and desires of the mother, disrupting the progenitive process and outcome (17–19). Stated differently, a woman's ideas or imagination (which I would extend to include her religious and political beliefs) were capable of marking the fetus, and they became public following its birth. Monsters, therefore, functioned as a form of rhetorical ammunition that was capable of rendering mothers and their convictions suspect, an understanding of pregnancy and progeny that proved extremely damaging for Hutchinson. Her case illustrates the possibilities of examining perceptions of motherhood in other historical periods and uncovering its contingent and diverse rhetorical forms.

3. The matrilineal traditions of the Cherokee, for example, merit examination as both the meaning of motherhood and the persuasive resources that stem from it are distinct from those examined in this project. In Cherokee culture, motherhood connoted "power rather than sentimentality," and mothers were accorded "honor," "prestige," civic responsibilities, and political standing (Perdue 101). Maternal rhetor Nanye-hi (Nancy Ward) would make an intriguing subject for a case study: She filled the crucial roles of War Woman (with complete dominion over prisoners), Beloved Woman, leader of the Women's Council (comprised of representatives from each Cherokee clan), and voting member of the Council of Chiefs at a difficult juncture in the late eighteenth and early nineteenth centuries. As the Cherokee nation struggled with equivocating government agents, encroaching white settlers, and shrinking lands, Ward participated actively in

tribal negotiations and at treaty conventions, consistently using motherhood to frame herself, her audience, and her arguments ("Nancy Ward," n.p.; McClary 354). A study of Nanye-hi might detail motherhood's meaning and rhetorical manifestation in Cherokee culture as well as the reception of her maternal appeals by the native and white audiences she addressed.

4. One of many promising possibilities is transmale pregnancy and birth, a phenomenon that pushes against conventional constructs of motherhood in fascinating ways. One might, for instance, focus on Thomas Beatie, who catapulted to fame in 2008 when his decision to bear a child (due to his wife Nancy's infertility) became public knowledge. Beatie used his moment in the spotlight to educate others, appearing in *People* and on the Oprah Winfrey show and publishing an essay and book about his pregnancy. The texts addressed a broad audience and explained Beatie's intersecting identities and civic standing clearly and accessibly: "I am transgender, legally male, and legally married to Nancy. Unlike those in same-sex marriages, domestic partnerships, or civil unions, Nancy and I are afforded the more than 1,100 federal rights of marriage. Sterilization is not a requirement for sex reassignment, so I decided to have chest reconstruction and testosterone therapy but kept my reproductive rights" ("Labor," n.p.). Once he decided to become pregnant, he halted bimonthly testosterone injections and, in short order, gave birth to a girl in 2008, a boy in 2009, and another son in 2010 ("Pregnant Man," n.p.). Transmale pregnancy unsettles the sexual binary, traditional gender constructs, and the Woman/Mother continuum in complicated ways. Although Beatie was born a woman, he no longer inhabits either the Woman or Mother categories comfortably; although legally a man, his pregnancy makes his "fit" within that category awkward as well. An analysis of maternal rhetorics might explore his self-presentation: Beatie consistently separated pregnancy and childbirth from being female and portrayed himself as a man, asserting that his decision to bear a child did not compromise his gender identity: "I was a man who was renting out his body to perform this one miraculous feat. I was not switching back to being a female; I was still, in my mind, fully male" (*Labor* 197). An analysis might also examine institutional responses to Beatie's pregnancy: The realms of insurance, medicine, politics, and law, for instance, often attempt to resolve the conceptual quandaries posed by transgender "motherhood" by insisting that one's sex assignment at birth permanently establishes gender, regardless of subsequent changes.

Works Cited

Acton, William. *The Functions and Disorders of the Reproductive Organs.* London: J. A. Churchill, 1857. Print.

Adams, Katherine, Michael Keene, and Melanie McKay. *Controlling Representations: Depictions of Women in a Mainstream Newspaper, 1900–1950.* Cresskill: Hampton, 2009. Print.

Ahmann, Mathew, ed. *The New Negro.* New York: Biblo and Tannen, 1969. Print.

Allen, Paula Gunn. *The Sacred Hoop: Recovering the Feminine in American Indian Traditions.* Boston: Beacon, 1992. Print.

Altman, Meryl, and Keith Nightenhelser. "Review: Thomas Lacqueur, *Making Sex.*" *Postmodern Culture* 2 (1992): n.p. Print.

Applegarth, Risa. "Genre, Location, and Mary Austin's *Ethos.*" *Rhetoric Society Quarterly* 41 (2011): 41–63. Print.

Aristotle. *On Rhetoric: A Theory of Civic Discourse.* Ed. George Kennedy. New York: Oxford UP, 1991. Print.

Aristotle's Masterpiece: The Secrets of Nature Displayed. London: J. Coker, 1900. Web. 20 March 2012. <http://www.exclassics.com/arist/ariintro.htm>.

Arsenault, Raymond. *Freedom Riders: 1961 and the Struggle for Racial Justice.* New York: Oxford UP, 2006. Print.

Aune, David. "Review of Thomas Lacqueur's *Making Sex.*" *Journal of Early Christian Studies* 1.3 (1993): 336–38. Print.

Baker, Paula. "The Domestication of Politics: Women and American Political Society, 1780–1920." *American Historical Review* 89 (1984): 620–47. Print.

Barthes, Roland. "Change the Object Itself: Mythology Today." Image, Music, Text. New York: Hill and Wang, 1977. 165–69. Print.

———. *Image, Music, Text.* New York: Hill and Wang, 1977. Print.

———. *Mythologies.* Trans. Annette Lavers. New York: Hill and Wang, 1972. Print.

———. "The Photographic Message." *Image, Music, Text.* New York: Hill and Wang, 1977. 15–31. Print.

———. "The Rhetoric of the Image." *Image, Music, Text.* New York: Hill and Wang, 1977. 32–51. Print.

———. *S/Z.* Trans. Richard Miller. New York: Hill and Wang, 1974. Print.

Bassin, Donna, Margaret Honey, and Meryle Kaplan. Introduction. Bassin, Honey, and Kaplan 1–25. Print.

———, eds. *Representations of Motherhood.* New Haven: Yale UP, 1994. Print.

Bay, Mia. *To Tell the Truth Freely: The Life of Ida B. Wells.* New York: Hill and Wang, 2009. Print.

Beatie, Thomas. "Labor of Love." Advocate April 2008. Web. 1 July 2010. <http://www.advocate.com/Society/Commentary/Labor_of_Love/>.

———. *Labor of Love: The Story of One Man's Extraordinary Pregnancy.* Berkeley: Seal, 2008. Print.

Bone, Jennifer Emerling. "When Publics Collide: Margaret Sanger's Argument for Birth Control and the Rhetorical Breakdown of Barriers." *Women's Studies in Communication* 33 (2010): 16–33. Print.

Bowers, Toni. *The Politics of Motherhood: British Writing and Culture, 1680–1760.* Cambridge: Cambridge UP, 1996. Print.

Branch, Taylor. *At Canaan's Edge: America in the King Years, 1965–68.* New York: Simon and Schuster, 2006. Print.

———. *Pillar of Fire: America in the King Years, 1963–65.* New York: Simon and Schuster, 1998. Print.

Buchanan, Lindal. *Regendering Delivery: The Fifth Canon and Antebellum Women Rhetors.* Carbondale: Southern Illinois UP, 2005. Print.

———. "A Study of Maternal Rhetoric: Anne Hutchinson, Monstrous Births, and the Antinomian Controversy." *Rhetoric Review* 25.3 (2006): 239–59. Print.

Buchanan, Lindal, and Kathleen Ryan, eds. *Walking and Talking Feminist Rhetorics: Landmark Essays and Controversies.* West Lafayette: Parlor, 2010. Print.

Bush, George. "Remarks by the President at Signing of the Unborn Victims of Violence Act of 2004." *Office of the Press Secretary.* 1 April 2004. Web. 15 March 2006.

Butler, Paul. *Out of Style: Reanimating Stylistic Study in Composition and Rhetoric.* Logan: Utah State UP, 2008. Print.

Cadogan, William. *Essay upon Nursing and the Management of Children from Birth to Three Years of Age.* 1748. Reprinted in Morwenna and John Rendle-Short, *The Father of Child Care: Life of William Cadogan.* Bristol: Wright, 1966. Print.

Campbell, Karlyn Kohrs. *Man Cannot Speak for Her: A Critical Study of Early Feminist Rhetoric.* Vol. 1. New York: Greenwood, 1989. Print.

Carson, Clayborne. *In Struggle: SNCC and the Black Awakening of the 1960s.* Cambridge: Harvard UP, 1995. Print.

———, ed. *The Student Voice, 1960–1965: Periodical of the Student Nonviolent Coordinating Committee.* Westport: Meckler, 1990. Print.

Casey, Patricia, ed. "Ninth Annual Review of Gender and Sexuality Law: Health Care Law Chapter: Abortion." *Georgetown Journal of Gender and the Law* 9 (2008): 1097. Print.

Center for American Women and Politics. "Fact Sheet: Women in the U.S. Congress, 1917–2007." *National Information Bank on Women in Public Office.* Eagleton Institute of Politics. Rutgers University. January 2007. Web. 6 February 2007. <http://www.cawp.rutgers.edu/Facts2.html>.

Chandler, Daniel. *Semiotics: The Basics.* 2nd ed. London: Routledge, 2007. Print.

Chesler, Ellen. *Woman of Valor: Margaret Sanger and the Birth Control Movement in America.* New York: Simon and Schuster, 1992. Print.

Clapp, Elizabeth. *Mothers of All Children: Women Reformers and the Rise of Juvenile Courts in Progressive Era America.* University Park: Penn State UP, 1998. Print.

Collier-Thomas, Bettye, and V. P. Franklin. *Sisters in the Struggle: African American Women in the Civil Rights-Black Power Movement.* New York: New York UP, 2001. Print.

Collins, Patricia Hill. *Black Feminist Thought: Knowledge, Consciousness, and the Politics of Empowerment.* New York: Routledge, 1990. Print.

———. "Shifting the Center: Race, Class, and Feminist Theorizing about Motherhood." Bassin, Honey, and Kaplan 56–74. Print.

Collins, Vicki. "The Speaker Respoken: Rhetoric as Feminist Methodology." *College English* 61 (1999): 545–71. Print.

Committee on the Judiciary. *Laci and Conner's Law: Report with Dissenting Views on H.R. 1997.* House of Representatives. 108th Cong., 2nd sess. H.R. Rep. No. 108–420, Pt. 1. (11 February 2004). Print.

Condit, Celeste. *Decoding Abortion Rhetoric: Communicating Social Change.* Chicago: U of Illinois P, 1990. Print.

Conway, Jill. "Perspectives on the History of Women's Education in the United States." *History of Education Quarterly* 14 (1974): 1–12. Print.

Crawford, Vicki L., Jacqueline Anne Rouse, and Barbara Woods, eds. *Women in the Civil Rights Movement: Trailblazers and Torchbearers, 1941–1965.* Bloomington: Indiana UP, 1993. Print.

Crenshaw, Kimberlé. "Mapping the Margins: Intersectionality, Identity Politics, and Violence against Women of Color." *Stanford Law Review* 43 (1991): 1241–99. Print.

Crier, Catherine. *A Deadly Game: The Untold Story of the Scott Peterson Investigation.* New York: Harper Collins, 2005. Print.

"Crisis of American Families and the Bias against Mothers." *MomsRising.Org.* Web. 6 February 2010.

Curran, William. "An Historical Perspective on the Law of Personality and Status with Special Regard to the Human Fetus and the Rights of Women." *Health and Society* 61 (1983): 58–75. Print.

Daniels, Cynthia. *At Women's Expense: State Power and the Politics of Fetal Rights.* Cambridge: Harvard UP, 1993. Print.

"Diane Nash." *The King Encyclopedia.* Stanford University. Web. 16 March 2008. <http://www.stanford.edu/group/King/about_king/encyclopedia/nash_diane.htm>.

"Dianne Nash Ready to Start Serving 2 Year Prison Sentence." *Jackson (MS) Advocate* 1: 21 (12 May 1962): 1, 6. Print.

DiQuinzio, Patrice. *The Impossibility of Motherhood: Feminism, Individualism, and the Problem of Mothering.* New York: Routledge, 1999. Print.

———. "Love and Reason in the Public Sphere: Maternalist Civic Engagement and the Dilemma of Difference." Meagher and DiQuinzio 227–46. Print.

Dolmage, Jay, and Cynthia Lewiecki-Wilson. "Refiguring Rhetorica: Linking Feminist Rhetoric and Disability Studies." Schell and Rawson 23–38. Print.

Donawerth, Jane. *Conversational Rhetoric: The Rise and Fall of a Women's Tradition, 1600–1900.* Carbondale: Southern Illinois UP, 2012. Print.

Dow, Bonnie J., and M. B. Tonn. "'Feminine Style' and Political Judgment in the Rhetoric of Ann Richards." *Quarterly Journal of Speech* 79 (1993): 286–302. Print.

DuBois, Ellen Carol. *Feminism and Suffrage: The Emergence of an Independent Women's Movement in America, 1848–1869.* Ithaca: Cornell UP, 1999. Print.

———. "Politics and Culture in Women's History." *Feminist Studies* 8 (1980): 26–64. Print.

Duden, Barbara. *Disembodying Women: Perspective on Pregnancy and the Unborn.* Trans. Lee Hoinacki. Cambridge: Harvard UP, 1993. Print.

Enoch, Jessica. *Refiguring Rhetorical Education: Women Teaching African American, Native American, and Chicano/a Students, 1865–1911.* Carbondale: Southern Illinois UP, 2008. Print.

Enos, Theresa, ed. *Encyclopedia of Rhetoric and Composition: Communication from Ancient Times to the Information Age.* New York: Routledge, 2010. Print.

Enstad, Nan. *Ladies of Labor, Girls of Adventure: Working Women, Popular Culture, and Labor Politics at the Turn of the Twentieth Century.* New York: Columbia UP, 1999. Print.

Epstein, Julia. "The Pregnant Imagination, Women's Bodies, and Fetal Rights." Greenfield and Barash 111–37. Print.

Fabj, Valeria. "Motherhood as Political Voice: The Rhetoric of the Mothers of Plaza de Mayo." *Communication Studies* 44 (1993): 1–18. Print.

Foss, Karen, and Kathy Domenici. "Haunting Argentina: Synecdoche in the Protests of the Mothers of the Plaza de Mayo." *Quarterly Journal of Speech* 87 (2001): 237–58. Print.

Foucault, Michel. *The Archeology of Knowledge and the Discourse on Language.* New York: Vintage, 1982. Print.

———. *The History of Sexuality. Volume I: An Introduction.* Trans. Robert Hurley. New York: Pantheon, 1978. Print.

———. "Truth and Knowledge." *Power/Knowledge: Selected Interviews and Other Writings, 1972–77.* New York: Pantheon, 1980. 109–33. Print.

"Fourteenth Amendment." *The U.S. Constitution.* The Legal Information Institute, Cornell University. Web. 25 July 2009. <http://www.law.cornell.edu/constitution/amendmentxiv>.

Franks, Angela. *Margaret Sanger's Eugenic Legacy: The Control of Female Fertility.* Jefferson: McFarland, 2005. Print.

Gage, John. "Enthymeme." Enos 223–25. Print.

Giddings, Paula. *Ida: A Sword among Lions.* New York: Amistad, 2008. Print.

———. *When and Where I Enter: The Impact of Black Women on Race and Sex in America.* New York: William Morrow, 1984. Print.

Gilbert, Scott. "Medical Implications of Developmental Biology." *Developmental Biology.* 8th ed. New York: Sinauer, 2006. Print.

Ginzberg, Lori. *Women and the Work of Benevolence.* New Haven: Yale UP, 1990. Print.

Glenn, Cheryl. "*Comment:* Truth, Lies, and Method: Revisiting Feminist Historiography." Buchanan and Ryan 462–64. Print.

———. *Rhetoric Retold: Regendering the Tradition from Antiquity through the Renaissance.* Carbondale: Southern Illinois UP, 1997. Print.

———. *Unspoken: The Rhetoric of Silence.* Carbondale: Southern Illinois UP, 2004. Print.

Glenn, Evelyn Nakano. "Social Constructions of Mothering: A Thematic Overview." Glenn, Change, and Forcey 1–29. Print.

Glenn, Evelyn Nakano, Grace Change, and Linda Forcey, eds. *Mothering: Ideology, Experience, and Agency.* New York: Routledge, 1994. Print.

Gordon, Linda. *Dorothea Lange: A Life beyond Limits.* New York: Norton, 2009. Print.

———. "Putting Children First: Women, Maternalism, and Welfare in the Early Twentieth Century." Kerber and Sklar 63–86. Print.

———. *Woman's Body, Woman's Right: A Social History of Birth Control in America.* New York: Grossman, 1976. Print.

Gray, Madeline. *Margaret Sanger: A Biography of the Champion of Birth Control.* New York: Richard Marek, 1979. Print.

Greenfield, Susan, and Carol Barash, eds. *Inventing Maternity: Politics, Science, and Literature, 1650–1865.* Lexington: UP of Kentucky, 1999. Print.

Gutiérrez, Elena. "We Will No Longer Be Silent or Invisible: Latinas Organizing for Reproductive Justice." O'Reilly, *Maternal Theory* 683–704. Print.

Halberstam, David. *The Children.* New York: Random House, 1998. Print.

Halloran, Michael. "Aristotle's Concept of Ethos, or If Not His Somebody Else's." *Rhetoric Review* 1 (1982): 58–63. Print.

Hampton, Henry, and Steven Fayer, eds. *Voices of Freedom: An Oral History of the Civil Rights Movement from the 1950s through the 1980s.* New York: Bantam, 1991. Print.

Hardy, Sarah, and Caroline Wiedmer, eds. *Motherhood and Space: Configurations of the Maternal through Politics, Home, and the Body.* New York: Palgrave Macmillan, 2005. Print.

Hariman, Robert, and John Louis Lucaites. "Public Identity and Collective Memory in U.S. Iconic Photography: The Image of 'Accidental Napalm.'" *Critical Studies in Media Communication* 20 (2003): 35–66. Print.

Harris, Leslie. "Motherhood, Race, and Gender: The Rhetoric of Women's Antislavery Activism in the *Liberty Bell* Giftbooks." *Women's Studies in Communication* 32.3 (2009): 293–319. Print.

Harvey, William. *The Works of William Harvey.* Trans. Robert Willis. London: Sydenham Society, 1965. Print.

Hayden, Sara. "Family Metaphors and the Nation: Promoting a Politics of Care through the Million Mom March." *Quarterly Journal of Speech* 89 (2003): 196–215. Print.

———. "Revitalizing the Debate between <Life> and <Choice>: The 2004 March for Women's Lives." *Communication and Critical/Cultural Studies* 6 (2009): 111–31. Print.

Helsley, Sherri. "Kairos." Enos 371. Print.

Higginbotham, Evelyn. *Righteous Discontent: The Women's Movement in the Black Baptist Church, 1880–1920.* Cambridge: Harvard UP, 1993. Print.

Hirsch, Marianne, and Evelyn Fox Keller, eds. *Conflicts in Feminism.* New York: Routledge, 1990. Print.

Hobbs, Catherine, ed. *Nineteenth-Century Women Learn to Write.* Charlottesville: UP of Virginia, 1995. Print.

Houck, Davis W., and David E. Dixon. *Women and the Civil Rights Movement, 1954–1965.* Oxford: UP of Mississippi, 2009. Print.

House of Representatives. *Congressional Record.* Proceedings and Debates of the 108th Congress, 2nd Session. Vol. 150: 22 (26 February 2004): H635–701. Print.

Hull, N. E. H., and Peter Hoffer. *Roe v. Wade: The Abortion Rights Controversy in American History.* Lawrence: UP of Kansas, 2001. Print.

Hyde, Michael. Introduction: "Rhetorically, We Dwell." Hyde, xiii–xxviii. Print.

———, ed. *The Ethos of Rhetoric.* Columbia: U of South Carolina P, 2004. Print.

Jacob, Krista, ed. *Abortion under Attack: Women on the Challenges Facing Choice.* Berkeley: Seal, 2006. Print.

Johnson, Nan. "Ethos." Enos 243–45. Print.

———. *Gender and Rhetorical Space in American Life, 1866–1910.* Carbondale: Southern Illinois UP, 2002. Print.

Jones, J. Charles. "Rock Hill and Charlotte Sit-ins." *Civil Rights Movement Veterans.* 2003. Web. 4 January 2009. <http://www.crmvet.org/info/rockhill.htm>.

Kaplan, E. Ann. *Motherhood and Representation: The Mother in Popular Culture and Melodrama.* New York: Routledge, 1992. Print.

Katz, Esther, ed. *The Selected Papers of Margaret Sanger. Volume 1: The Woman Rebel, 1900–1928*. Urbana: U of Illinois P, 2003. Print.

Kerber, Linda. "Separate Spheres, Female Worlds, Woman's Place: The Rhetoric of Women's History." *Journal of American History* 75 (1988): 9–39. Print.

———. *Women of the Republic: Intellect and Ideology in Revolutionary America*. Chapel Hill: U of North Carolina P, 1980. Print.

Kerber, Linda, and Kathryn Kish Sklar, eds. *U.S. History as Women's History: New Feminist Essays*. Chapel Hill: U of North Carolina P, 1995. Print.

Kinser, Amber. *Motherhood and Feminism*. Berkeley: Seal, 2010. Print.

Kipp, Julie. *Romanticism, Maternity, and the Body Politic*. Cambridge: Cambridge UP, 2003. Print.

Kirkup, Gill, Linda Janes, Kathryn Woodward, and Fiona Hovenden, eds. *The Gendered Cyborg: A Reader*. London: Routledge, 1999. Print.

Kissling, Frances. "Is There Life after *Roe*? How to Think about the Fetus." Jacob 189–205. Print.

Kolodiejchuk, Brian. *Mother Teresa: Come Be My Light*. New York: Doubleday, 2007. Print.

Koven, Seth, and Sonya Michel. *Mothers of a New World: Maternalist Politics and the Origins of Welfare States*. New York: Routledge, 1993. Print.

Kress, Gunther, and Theo Van Leeuwen. *Reading Images: The Grammar of Visual Design*. London: Routledge, 1996. Print.

Kukla, Rebecca. *Mass Hysteria: Medicine, Culture, and Mother's Bodies*. New York: Rowman and Littlefield, 2005. Print.

Lade, Lawrence. *The Margaret Sanger Story and the Fight for Birth Control*. Garden City: Doubleday, 1955. Print.

Laqueur, Thomas. *Making Sex: Body and Gender from the Greeks to Freud*. Cambridge: Harvard UP, 1990. Print.

Ling, Peter J., and Sharon Monteith, eds. *Gender and the Civil Rights Movement*. Piscataway: Rutgers UP, 2004. Print.

Logan, Shirley Wilson. *"We Are Coming": The Persuasive Discourse of Nineteenth-Century Black Women*. Carbondale: Southern Illinois UP, 1999. Print.

Lorde, Audre. "The Master's Tools Will Never Dismantle the Master's House." *Sister Outsider: Essays and Speeches*. Berkeley: Crossing, 1984. 110–13. Print.

Lunsford, Andrea, ed. *Reclaiming Rhetorica: Women in the Rhetorical Tradition*. Pittsburgh: U of Pittsburgh P, 1995. Print.

Marable, Manning. *Race, Reform, and Rebellion: The Second Reconstruction and Beyond in Black America, 1945–2006*. 3rd ed. Jackson: UP of Mississippi, 2007. vPrint.

Martin, Emily. *The Woman in the Body: A Cultural Analysis of Reproduction*. 1987. Boston: Beacon, 2001. Print.

Marzilli, Alan. *Fetal Rights*. Philadelphia: Chelsea House, 2005. Print.

Mattingly, Carol. *Appropriate[ing] Dress: Women's Rhetorical Style in Nineteenth-Century America*. Carbondale: Southern Illinois UP, 2002. Print.

———. *Well-Tempered Women: Nineteenth-Century Temperance Rhetoric*. Carbondale: Southern Illinois UP, 1998. Print.

McCain, John. "McCain Introduces Palin as Running Mate: Transcript." 29 August 2008. *Washington Post*. Web. 30 August 2008.

McCann, Carole. *Birth Control Politics in the United States, 1916–1945*. Ithaca: Cornell UP, 1994. Print.

McClary, Ben Harris. "Nancy Ward: The Last Beloved Woman of the Cherokees." *Tennessee Historical Quarterly* 21 (1962): 352–64. Print.

McLaren, Angus. *Reproductive Rituals: The Perception of Fertility in England from the Sixteenth Century to the Nineteenth Century.* New York: Methuen, 1984. Print.

Meagher, Sharon, and Patrice DiQuinzio, eds. *Women and Children First: Feminism, Rhetoric, and Public Policy.* Albany: State U of New York P, 2005. Print.

Micciche, Laura. *Doing Emotion: Rhetoric, Writing, and Teaching.* Portsmouth: Heinemann, 2007. Print.

Miller, Hildy, and Lillian Bridwell-Bowles, eds. *Rhetorical Women: Roles and Representations.* Tuscaloosa: U of Alabama P, 2005. Print.

Miller, Susan. *Trust in Texts: A Different History of Rhetoric.* Carbondale: Southern Illinois UP, 2008. Print.

"Miss. Judge Halts Expectant Mother's Jail Try" (June 1962). Carson, *Student Voice,* 53, 56. Print.

Morgan, Lynn, and Meredith Michaels. *Fetal Subjects, Feminist Positions.* Philadelphia: U of Pennsylvania P, 1999. Print.

Mountford, Roxanne. *The Gendered Pulpit: Preaching in American Protestant Spaces.* Carbondale: Southern Illinois UP, 2003. Print.

"Nancy Ward." *Tennessee Encyclopedia of History and Culture.* Online edition. Knoxville: U of Tennessee P, 2002. 13 June 2010.

Nash [Bevel], Diane. "Inside the Sit-ins and Freedom Rides: Testimony of a Southern Student." Ahmann 43–60. Print.

——— "A Message from Diane Nash Bevel to Individuals and Organizations Working for Civil Rights." (30 April 1962). *Records of the Southern Christian Leadership Conference,* 1954–1970. Pt. 1. Ed. Randolph Boehm and Blair Hydrick. Microform. Bethesda: University Publications of America, 1995. Part 3, Reel 4, Box 126 (0769), 123:43. 1–3.

———. Telephone interview. 4 May 2008.

"Nash, Diane." *King Encyclopedia.* Stanford University. Web. 20 June 2008.

Nguyen, Cindy. "Interpellation." *University of Chicago: Theories of Media: Keywords Glossary.* Web. 1 July 2011.

Norat, Gisela. "Women Staging Coups through Mothering." O'Reilly, *Feminist Mothering* 219–41. Print.

Olson, Lynne. *Freedom's Daughters: The Unsung Heroines of the Civil Rights Movement from 1830 to 1970.* New York: Scribner, 2002. Print.

O'Reilly, Andrea. *Mother Outlaws: Theories and Practices of Empowered Motherhood.* Toronto: Women's Press, 2004. Print.

———, ed. *Feminist Mothering.* Albany: State U of New York P, 2008. Print.

———, ed. *Maternal Theory: Essential Readings.* Toronto: Demeter, 2007. Print.

Palin, Sarah. Convention Speech. Republican National Convention. 3 September 2008. *New York Times.* Web. 4 Sept. 2008.

Park, Katherine, and Robert Nye. "Destiny Is Anatomy." *New Republic* 18 February 1991, 53–57. Print.

"A Particular Description of the Parts and Instruments of Generation, Both in Men and Women." *Aristotle's Masterpiece: The Secrets of Nature Displayed.* London: J. Coker & Co, 1900. Web. 20 March 2012. <http://www.exclassics.com/arist/arist6.htm>.

Perdue, Theda. *Cherokee Women: Gender and Culture Change, 1700–1835.* Lincoln: U of Nebraska P, 1998. Print.

Petchesky, Rosalind. *Abortion and Woman's Choice: The State, Sexuality, and Reproductive Freedom.* Rev. ed. Boston: Northeastern UP, 1990. Print.

———. "Foetal Images: The Power of Visual Culture in the Politics of Reproduction." Kirkup et al. 171–92. Print.

"Pregnant Man Thomas Beatie Expecting THIRD Child." *Huffington Post.* 10 February 2010. Web. 21 July 2010.

Ratcliffe, Krista. *Anglo-American Feminist Challenges to the Rhetorical Traditions: Virginia Woolf, Mary Daly, Adrienne Rich.* Carbondale: Southern Illinois UP, 1996. Print.

———. *Rhetorical Listening: Identification, Gender, Whiteness.* Carbondale: Southern Illinois UP, 2006. Print.

Reed, Miriam. *Margaret Sanger: Her Life in Her Words.* Fort Lee: Barricade, 2003. Print.

Return of the Freedom Riders, 50th Anniversary Reunion. Web. 15 July 2011. <http://ms50thfreedomridersreunion.org/>.

Reynolds, Nedra. "*Ethos* as Location: New Sites for Understanding Discursive Authority." *Rhetoric Review* 11 (1993): 325–38. Print.

Rich, Adrienne. *Of Woman Born: Motherhood as Experience and Institution.* 1976. New York: Norton, 1995. Print.

Richardson, Judy. "An Interview with Diane Nash." *Footsteps* 2.3 (May 2000): 24. Print.

Robnett, Belinda. *How Long? How Long? African-American Women in the Struggle for Civil Rights.* New York: Oxford UP, 1997. Print.

Ross, Rosetta. *Witnessing and Testifying: Black Women, Religion, and Civil Rights.* Minneapolis: Fortress, 2003. Print.

Roth, Rachel. *Making Women Pay: The Hidden Costs of Fetal Rights.* Ithaca: Cornell UP, 2000. Print.

Rousseau, Jean-Jacques. *Emile; or, Treatise on Education.* 1762. Trans. William Payne. New York: Prometheus, 2003. Print.

Royster, Jacqueline Jones. "Introduction: Marking Trials in Studies of Race, Gender, and Culture." Royster and Simpkins 1–14. Print.

———. *Traces of a Stream: Literacy and Social Change among African American Women.* Pittsburgh: U of Pittsburgh P, 2000. Print.

Royster, Jacqueline Jones, and Ann Marie Simpkins, eds. *Calling Cards: Theories and Practice in the Study of Race, Gender, and Culture.* Albany: State U of New York P, 2005. Print.

Ruddick, Sara. *Maternal Thinking: Toward a Politics of Peace.* Boston: Beacon, 1989.

Saletan, William. *Bearing Right: How Conservatives Won the Abortion War.* Berkeley: U of California P, 2003. Print.

Sanger, Margaret. *Appeals from American Mothers.* New York: New York Women's Publishing, 1921. *Margaret Sanger Papers: Smith College Collections.* Microfilm edition. Reel S76: 238853.

———. *English Methods of Birth Control* [pamphlet]. 1915. *Margaret Sanger Papers: Smith College Collections.* Microfilm edition. Reel S76: 236708.

———. *Family Limitation.* 1914. *Margaret Sanger Papers: Smith College Collections.* Microfilm edition. Reel S76: 238157.

———. File no. 4, "1916, . . . federal trial." Box 210. Margaret Sanger Papers. Manuscript Division. Library of Congress. Washington, D.C.

———. File no. 5, "April 1916–Jan. 1917 . . . Miscellaneous Clippings, 1916–1920." Box 211. Margaret Sanger Papers. Manuscript Division. Library of Congress. Washington, D.C.

———. File no. 6, "1916–1926 . . . early trials and miscellaneous history." Box 212. Margaret Sanger Papers. Manuscript Division. Library of Congress. Washington, D.C.

———. File no. 7, "Oct. 1916–March 1917 Trial." Box 211. Margaret Sanger Papers. Manuscript Division. Library of Congress. Washington, D.C.

———. *Margaret Sanger: An Autobiography*. 1938. Reprint, New York: Cooper Square, 1999. Print.

———. "A Message to Mothers." 1916. "Early printed articles by and about Margaret Sanger." Box 218. Margaret Sanger Papers. Manuscript Division. Library of Congress. Washington, D.C.

———. "Notes on Address Contemplating Trial re Woman Rebel." 1916. *Papers of Margaret Sanger*. Microfilm edition. Reel 130: 342.

———. *Papers of Margaret Sanger*. Microfilm edition. 1977. Library of Congress. Washington, D.C.

———. Papers: Manuscript Division. Library of Congress. Washington, D.C.

———. *Papers: Smith College Collections and Collected Documents Series*. Microfilm edition. Bethesda: University Publications of America, 1996, 1997.

———. *Papers on Appeal*. New York Supreme Court, Appellate Division. 1917. *Margaret Sanger Papers: Smith College Collections*. Microfilm edition. Reel S69: 239828.

———. Press Sheet and "Stills" from motion picture, "Birth Control," 1916. Box 247. Margaret Sanger Papers. Manuscript Division. Library of Congress. Washington, D.C.

———. Publisher's note. *Woman Rebel* (First Issue) March 1914, 1. Print.

———. "Stump Speech." April 1916. *Papers of Margaret Sanger*. Microfilm edition. Library of Congress. Washington, D.C. Reel 129:12.

———. "Woman, Morality, and Birth Control." 1916. New York: New York Women's Publishing, 1922. *Margaret Sanger Papers: Smith College Collections*. Microfilm edition. Reel S76: 236711.

Schell, Eileen, and K. Rawson, eds. *Rhetorica in Motion: Feminist Rhetorical Methods and Methodologies*. Pittsburgh: U of Pittsburgh P, 2010. Print.

Schiappa, Edward. *Defining Reality: Definitions and the Politics of Meaning*. Carbondale: Southern Illinois UP, 2003. Print.

Schlib, John. *Rhetorical Refusals: Defying Audiences' Expectations*. Carbondale: Southern Illinois UP, 2007. Print.

Scott, Joan W. *Gender and the Politics of History*. 1989. Rev. ed. New York: Columbia UP, 1999. Print.

Senate. *Congressional Record*. Proceedings and Debates of the 108th Congress, 2nd Session. Vol. 150: 39 (25 March 2004): S3119–98. Print.

Sharer, Wendy. *Voice and Vote: Women's Organizations and Public Literacy, 1915–1930*. Carbondale: Southern Illinois UP, 2004. Print.

Silverman, Kaja. *The Subject of Semiotics*. New York: Oxford UP, 1983. Print.

Skinner, Carolyn. "'The Purity of Truth': Nineteenth-Century American Women Physicians Write about Delicate Topics." *Rhetoric Review* 26 (2007): 103–19. Print.

———. "'She Will Have Science': Ethos and Audience in Mary Gove's *Lectures to Ladies*." *Rhetoric Society Quarterly* 39 (2009): 240–59. Print.

Snitow, Ann. "Feminism and Motherhood: An American Reading." *Feminist Review* 40 (1992): 32–51. Print.

———. "A Gender Diary." Hirsch and Fox Keller 9–43. Print.

Stadtman Tucker, Judith. "Rocking the Boat: Feminism and the Ideological Grounding of the Twenty-First Century Mothers' Movement." O'Reilly, *Feminist Mothering* 205–18. Print.

Stanton, Mary. *From Selma to Sorrow: The Life and Death of Viola Liuzzo*. Athens: U of Georgia P, 1998. Print.

"State Homicide Laws That Recognize Unborn Victims (Fetal Homicide)." *National Right to Life Committee* (NRLC.org.) 27 May 2011. Web. 30 July 2011.

Stearney, Lynn. "Feminism, Ecofeminism, and the Maternal Archetype: Motherhood as a Feminine Universal." *Communication Quarterly* 42 (1994): 145–59. Print.

Stringer, Rebecca. "Prenatal Politics: Reflections on the USA's Unborn Victims of Violence Act." Refereed Proceedings of the Australasian Political Studies Association. Dunedin: U of Otago, 2005. Print.

Supreme Court. *Gonzales v. Carhart* Decision, 18 April 2007. *FindLaw.com*. Web. 30 April 2007.

———. *Roe v Wade* Decision, 22 January 1973. *TouroLaw.edu*. Web. 15 March 2006. <http://www.tourolaw.edu/patch/Roe/>.

"Supreme Court Hears Abortion Arguments." *CBSNews.com*. 8 November 2006. Web. 6 February 2007.

"Supreme Court OKs Abortion Procedure Ban." *Yahoo!News.com*. 18 April 2007. Web. 30 April 2007.

Sutherland, Christine Mason, and Rebecca Sutcliffe, eds. *The Changing Tradition: Women in the History of Rhetoric*. Calgary: U of Calgary P, 1999. Print.

Swerdlow, Amy. *Women Strike for Peace: Traditional Motherhood and Radical Politics in the 1960s*. Chicago: U of Chicago P, 1993. Print.

Theoharis, Jeanne. "Diane Nash." *Encyclopedia of Black Women in America*. Ed. Darlene Hine. New York: Carlson, 1993. 834–36. Print.

Thompson, Julie. *Mommy Queerest: Contemporary Rhetorics of Lesbian Maternal Identity*. Boston: U of Massachusetts P, 2002. Print.

Toner, Robin. "Clinton, Pelosi Play Political Mom Card." 29 January 2007. Web. *San Diego Union Tribune*. 4 June 2007.

Tonn, Mari Boor. "Militant Motherhood: Labor's Mary Harris 'Mother' Jones." *Quarterly Journal of Speech* 82 (1996): 1–21. Print.

Traister, Rebecca. "Morality Play." Jacob 227–40. Print.

Tronto, Joan. *Moral Boundaries: A Political Argument for an Ethic of Care*. New York: Routledge, 1993. Print.

Ullman, Sharon. "Review Essay: Making Sense of Sex." *Radical History Review* 52 (1992): 114–20. Print.

Van Leeuwen, Theo. *Introducing Social Semiotics*. London: Routledge, 2005. Print.

Warner, Judith. "The Motherhood Religion." O'Reilly, *Maternal Theory* 705–21. Print.

Warnke, Georgia. "Race, Gender, and Antiessentialist Politics." *Signs* 35 (2005): 93–116. Print.

Weaver, Richard. *The Ethics of Rhetoric*. 1953. South Bend: Gateway, 1977. Print.

Wellman, Carl. "The Concept of Fetal Rights." *Law and Philosophy* 21 (2002): 65–93. Print.

Welter, Barbara. "The Cult of True Womanhood: 1820–1860." *American Quarterly* 18 (1966): 151–74. Print.

Wertheimer, Molly, ed. *Listening to Their Voices: The Rhetorical Activities of Historical Women*. Columbia: U of South Carolina P, 1997. Print.

Westmoreland-White, Michael. "Diane Nash (1938–), Unsung Heroine of the Civil Rights Movement." *Pilgrim Pathways: Notes for a Diaspora People*. Web. 21 Oct. 2012.

Wolff, Kristina. "Strategic Essentialism." *Blackwell Encyclopedia of Sociology*. New York: Wiley-Blackwell, 2007. 10: 4789–91. Print.

Working Group on Women and Human Rights. "Background Briefing on Intersectionality." *Center for Women's Global Leadership*. Rutgers University. Web. 3 July 2011.

Worsham, Lynn. "Going Postal: Pedagogic Violence and the Schooling of Emotions." *Journal of Advanced Composition* 18 (1998): 213–45. Print.

Yoos, George. "Logos." Enos 410–14. Print.

Young, Andrew. *An Easy Burden: The Civil Rights Movement and the Transformation of America*. New York: HarperCollins, 1996. Print.

Zinn, Howard. *SNCC: The New Abolitionists*. Boston: Beacon, 1964. Print.

Index

Page numbers in italics denote illustrations.

Lindal Buchanan is an assistant professor of English and women's studies at Old Dominion University. She is the author of *Regendering Delivery: The Fifth Canon and Antebellum Women Rhetors* and a coeditor (with Kathleen J. Ryan) of *Walking and Talking Feminist Rhetorics: Landmark Essays and Controversies*. She has published in *Rhetoric Review*, *Rhetorica*, and *Rhetoric Society Quarterly* and was the recipient of the 2003 Kneupper Award.

Studies in Rhetorics and Feminisms

Studies in Rhetorics and Feminisms seeks to address the interdisciplinarity that rhetorics and feminisms represent. Rhetorical and feminist scholars want to connect rhetorical inquiry with contemporary academic and social concerns, exploring rhetoric's relevance to current issues of opportunity and diversity. This interdisciplinarity has already begun to transform the rhetorical tradition as we have known it (upper-class, agonistic, public, and male) into regendered, inclusionary rhetorics (democratic, dialogic, collaborative, cultural, and private). Our intellectual advancements depend on such ongoing transformation.

Rhetoric, whether ancient, contemporary, or futuristic, always inscribes the relation of language and power at a particular moment, indicating who may speak, who may listen, and what can be said. The only way we can displace the traditional rhetoric of masculine-only, public performance is to replace it with rhetorics that are recognized as being better suited to our present needs. We must understand more fully the rhetorics of the non-Western tradition, of women, of a variety of cultural and ethnic groups. Therefore, Studies in Rhetorics and Feminisms espouses a theoretical position of openness and expansion, a place for rhetorics to grow and thrive in a symbiotic relationship with all that feminisms have to offer, particularly when these two fields intersect with philosophical, sociological, religious, psychological, pedagogical, and literary issues.

The series seeks scholarly works that both examine and extend rhetoric, works that span the sexes, disciplines, cultures, ethnicities, and sociocultural practices as they intersect with the rhetorical tradition. After all, the recent resurgence of rhetorical studies has been not so much a discovery of new rhetorics as a recognition of existing rhetorical activities and practices, of our newfound ability and willingness to listen to previously untold stories.

The series editors seek both high-quality traditional and cutting-edge scholarly work that extends the significant relationship between rhetoric and feminism within various genres, cultural contexts, historical periods, methodologies, theoretical positions, and methods of delivery (e.g., film and hypertext to elocution and preaching).

Queries and submissions:
Professor Cheryl Glenn, Editor
    E-mail: cjg6@psu.edu
Professor Shirley Wilson Logan, Editor
    E-mail: slogan@umd.edu

Studies in Rhetorics and Feminisms
Department of English
142 South Burrowes Bldg.
Penn State University
University Park, PA 16802-6200

Other Books in the Studies in Rhetorics and Feminisms Series